AUTHORITY AND OBEDIENCE IN THE CHURCH

Milton L. Rudnick

Lutheran Education Association
7400 Augusta Street
Chicago, Illinois 60305

Art work by

Katherine Berwald

To
Carlene
Ps. 25:6

Preface

When a church body is in the throes of an authority crisis its educators are inevitably implicated. As teachers of the church we are responsible for interpreting the church to those whom we serve as well as to others. People young and old ask questions about what is going on. They ask us to share our understanding of the problems and our evaluation of what is being said and done. We owe them a thoughtful and informed response. Answers, in the sense of solutions, are hard to come by. The issues are numerous and authority is only one of them. Furthermore, they are exceedingly sensitive and complex issues. Conflicting opinions abound. In the Lutheran family, for example, who really knows what has happened in the Missouri Synod, what is happening, or what ought to happen? Each commentator on authority and obedience speaks out of his or her particular experience and bias. Some claim to have penetrated to the core of the problem, to have identified the "real issue," and to have devised a promising solution. However, as we look further we find that the data can be assembled and interpreted in other equally plausible ways and that a good case can be made for other proposed solutions.

If we can not offer solutions to all the problems on authority and obedience, perhaps we can provide useful information and perspective as well as some questions for reflection and discussion. Perhaps we can draw up some helpful distinctions and definitions to aid concerned persons in formulating or clarifying their own positions. This, at least, is the modest goal of this book with reference to the matter of authority and obedience in the church.

In the course of the controversy which convulses the Lutheran Church-Missouri Synod a great deal is said about authority. Some are accused of abusing church authority. Others are accused of defying legitimate church authority. What becomes obvious to the alert observer is that the principals in the controversy have very different ideas of what church authority is and how it ought to be exercised and obeyed. One approach to the subject might be to analyze and evaluate statements about church authority made by spokespersons of various positions. However, this is not what is undertaken here. I do not believe that what the Missouri Synod needs at this point is yet another display of its disagreements and misunderstandings. Consequently, I have chosen to focus attention, not on the current arguments about church authority in the LC-MS, but rather on what Scripture and the Lutheran Confessions have to say on the subject. I have attempted to state as clearly and simply as possible, not so much for the theologian as for the Lutheran educator and pastor as well as for the concerned lay person: (1) what the four basic kinds of church authority are, (2) how they relate to each other, and (3) the form of obedience appropriate to each.

No claim is made here either to originality, infallibility, or completeness. I have attempted to express with fidelity what the Bible and the Confessions teach. I have also offered some analysis and some opinions about how these teachings relate to our present situation. These are intended, not as dogmatic statements or final conclusions, but rather as relevant illustrations drawn from my own perception of what Scripture and the Confessions are saying to us today. I also try to indicate in several instances where and how others have come to different conclusions. This book is to be a discussion starter rather than a definitive interpretation, and I take comfort in this. Hopefully, in the course of the discussion and in the response of readers and critics my errors will be corrected and my limitations transcended.

In some respects, this is a very parochial book, written by a Missouri Synod Lutheran with examples taken from the experiences of that body. However, other readers, too, may find it relevant. Crises of authority and obedience are not confined to the Missouri Synod. The biblical and theological insights which are the heart of this presentation may also ring true to those of other confessional and ecclesiastical commitments and prove useful to them in responding to their own situations.

By way of acknowledgment I would like to express my appreciation to J. D. Weinhold and Kenneth Heinitz of the Lutheran Education Association for their editorial work. Their encouragement and suggestions have been most helpful. Rich Bimler, President of the L.E.A., has taken personal as well as official interest in the project and has been most supportive. David Schmiel read the manuscript and reacted to it. The theology faculty of Concordia Teachers College Seward, Nebraska invited me to share some of this material in the Regina Maehr Memorial Lectures for 1977. It was an experience made memorable by superb hospitality and stimulating discussion. Family and colleagues have stood by lovingly and patiently. I am grateful to all. However, responsibility for the basic thrust of this book as well as for its defects are mine alone.

Milton L. Rudnick
St. Paul, Minnesota

Abbreviations

References to the Lutheran Confessions cited throughout this book are from Theodore G. Tappert, trans. and ed., *The Book of Concord: the Confessions of the Evangelical Lutheran Church* (Saint Louis: Concordia Publishing House, c. 1959). Titles of the individual documents are abbreviated as follows:

A.C.	Augsburg Confession
Ap.	Apology of the Augsburg Confession
Ep.	Epitome of the Formula of Concord
F.C.	Formula of Concord
L.C.	Large Catechism
Tr.	Treatise on the Power and Primacy of the Pope
S.A.	Smalcald Articles
S.C.	Small Catechism
S.D.	Solid Declaration of the Formula of Concord

TABLE OF CONTENTS

evangelical
organizational
AUTHORITY
confessional
disciplinary

Chapter I

Introduction

As the title indicates, this is a study of authority and obedience *in the church.* The focus is narrow but basic. No attempt will be made to consider questions of authority and obedience in the home, the school, employment, the military, or the government. These are extremely inportant areas, and problems in these areas deserve attention. Except for an occasional and incidental reference, however, this discussion will not deal with them. Rather, its scope is restricted to those issues of authority and obedience which relate directly to the church.

The term "church" itself requires definition, since it is used in a variety of ways. In its broadest and most basic sense, the church is the whole people of God, all who belong to Him and to one another through faith in Jesus Christ. It is the body of Christ, the *Una Sancta.* This one, universal community of faith is manifested in any number of local assemblies. Believers in various places gather in groups to worship their Lord and to work for Him. These groups, or congregations, are also properly designated as "churches." What makes a group of people in a given place the church is not merely their decision to apply that term to themselves, nor a building of a certain design, nor a constitution, nor a professional leader, but rather a common faith in Jesus Christ generated and sustained by the proper use of His Word and Sacraments. For the church is not a human organization or creation, but the product of God's own work through the Holy Spirit in the means of grace.[1]

Several factors complicate the task of perceiving and defining the church. One is the impossibility of knowing precisely who the members are. Only true believers belong to Christ and to His church, but we have no way of knowing with certainty in any context who truly believes. We must take people at their word. Whoever confesses faith in Christ must be accepted as one of His own unless this confession is profoundly contradicted by something else that the person says or does. So any group which has and uses the Gospel in Word and Sacraments and professes faith in Christ is to be regarded as and related to as church, even though individuals in that group may be insincere or even apostate.

Another complicating factor is the existence of doctrinal differences and error. Obviously, not all Christians understand and express the message in similar or even compatible terms. There are serious disagreements among various denominations and subdivisions within denominational families. Furthermore, some who claim the name "Christian" and "church" have deviated so drastically from the faith that it is questionable that they are still part of the church. Such factors highlight the importance of the distinction between the true church and the empirical church, that is to say, between the spiritual fellowship of true believers and the external manifestations of the church—congregations, synods, denominations, federations, etc., which are also often designated as "church" but which, in fact, include persons and entire groups which are not part of the church in the strict sense of the term. Traditional Lutheran theological language refers to these two aspects of the church as the invisible and the visible churches.[2]

Whenever we think or talk about "the church" we are vulnerable to serious confusion if we lose sight of the distinction between the true church and its external manifestations. On the one hand, we deal with the various units of the empirical church as if they are the true church. For most practical purposes my congregation, my district, my synod are the church for me, for these are the manifestations of the Holy Christian Church with which I relate and work most closely. Consequently, when I consider matters such as authority and obedience in the church I consider them primarily as they appear in these contexts—the authority of the congregation and its ministries, the authority of synod and its leaders, and the forms of obedience which properly belong to these.

On the other hand, my vision is tragically narrow and blurred if I identify my external church organizations completely and exclusively with the church. Surely, the church is found in our congregations and synod. Hopefully, we are firmly committed to, and convinced of the truthfulness of, our confessions. However, we can be certain that false and unbelieving persons are also affiliated with our organization at every level and that the devil still works even through those among us who are true Christians. Furthermore, we can be certain that true Christians are found outside our organizational boundaries, also in churches which we judge to teach incorrectly on some points, and that authentic Christian assemblies exist and function elsewhere. In short, we must never forget that the Holy Christian Church, the true church, is a great family of which we are only one small part.

In any case, it is specifically *in the church* that we will explore the issues of authority and obedience.

As we prepare to do this it is important to note that the connotations of these terms in Scripture and the Confessions are in sharp contrast with those to which we are accustomed, i.e., those connotations which are conveyed by our culture.

To begin with the latter, it seems safe to say that in our culture the connotations of both "authority" and "obedience" are largely negative. In the interest of social organization, most will agree that some forms of authority are necessary, but they are regarded as necessary evils and limited as much as possible. Authority seems to signify repression or even oppression. It is seen as the enemy of freedom and personal fulfillment, and these are the values which are cherished most in our culture. Similarly, the connotations of "obedience" are also negative. The vision of obedience with which we are usually confronted is dismal and stifling. Obedience means squelching one's own desires and surrendering to those of another. Obedience is limiting and frustrating, even dehumanizing. It is the demeaning of self, perhaps even the destruction of self.

Reasons for these negative views of authority and obedience are not difficult to discover. One would be the rise in the last decade or so of the various psychological movements which emphasize the self, such as self-awareness, self-esteem, self-fulfillment, self-assertion. This is not the place nor am I the person to attempt a serious analysis of these movements. I will venture the opinion, however, that much of what is written on these themes, especially in the popular press, goes well beyond a wholesome and necessary appreciation of self to a celebration and advocacy of sinful selfishness. Even apart from this, it would seem inevitable that any widespread emphasis on the self with a high appreciation for autonomy and personal freedom would tend to diminish appreciation for authority and obedience, and may, in fact, be the antithesis of genuine authority and obedience.

In addition, recent history confronts us with shocking abuses of authority and corresponding atrocities committed in the name of obedience. The prison camps of Nazi Germany and Soviet Russia come to mind. More recently and closer to home were the massacres in South Viet Nam by American servicemen and the Watergate scandals—all in the name of obedience to authority. Stanley Milgram's psychological experiments reveal the willingness of a large percentage of subjects representing a cross-section of the population to perform morally reprehensible acts in obedience to authority.[3] Clearly, authority and obedience can take irresponsible and dangerous forms. Furthermore, as nation after nation capitulates to some form of totalitarianism with the subsequent loss of personal freedoms and escalating demands for unquestioning obedience to authority, we tend to shrink back from authority and obedience of any kind. Authority appears menacing. A posture of obedience and submissiveness is associated with victims of racism and chauvinism. Not respect for and obedience to authority, but self-assertion and even revolution are regarded by some as marks of the liberated and fulfilled person.

These negative attitudes toward various kinds of authority and obedience acquired from our culture may also color and distort our vision of authority and obedience in the church. We may approach the subject with a jaundiced eye. We may be convinced in advance that in the church, too, authority is a threat and obedience capitulation. To whatever extent this happens it is unfortunate. In the first place, authority and obedience in the church are radically different from their counterparts in the world. Although there are also some similarities with authority and obedience experienced elsewhere, the contrast is most striking. The definitions as well as the connotations of the terms convey some surprising and very positive elements. Consequently, it is important to approach the subject with an open mind and even with joyful expectation.

At this point it will be useful to make some distinctions and to formulate some general working definitions. A distinction is often made between personal authority and official authority. Personal authority is that which a person wields simply because of his knowledge or technical expertise or because of the high regard in which he is held by other people.[4] Thus, a highly respected micro-biologist announces to a community that its water supply is contaminated and that the water should be treated before drinking it. Many people will comply whether or not he has any official authority to require this of them. Official authority is that which a person possesses because of a special position into which he or she has been placed. Thus, the president of the United States has the authority to command the armed forces, not necessarily because he is more knowledgeable and skilled than others in these matters but simply because he is the president. In the church as well as elsewhere both personal and official authority are in evidence. In a congregation which I once served as pastor the most highly respected, and in some respects the most influential, member was not the pastor or the elected officers, but a humble dedicated layman through whose tireless and winsome witness many of the members had been gained for Christ and for the church.

"Authority" is often defined simply as the power to act. Generally implied in this is also the right to make decisions. Sometimes (but not in the church, as we shall see) authority also includes the right to command others. The element of duty is also often attached to authority. The person in authority not only may, but often should decide or act. Another way of stating the definition is in terms of privilege and responsibility, and this will be the form employed throughout this book. Authority is a privilege, an honor, a right to function in a special way. Legitimate authority of any kind is to be respected and revered because, ultimately, all legitimate authority is from God.

Every person with authority carries some of God's own dignity and is carrying out God's own purpose. Regardless of their personal inadequacies and unworthiness honor is still due those in authority. God has structured life in this world, and even in the next, in such a way that some people have authority over others. The reason for this is *not* to allow some to oppress and exploit others. Rather, those in authority are to protect, provide, lead, and uplift those over whom they exercise authority. Authority is a positive entity because of its divine origin and purpose. To whatever extent authority conforms to God's intention it is a blessing, not a curse, a source of security and well-being, not a threat. Those in authority, as God's agents, are accountable to Him. They are expected to function in the manner that He prescribes. For them to exercise their authority is not optional, but obligatory. In summary, then, authority is the divinely ordained privilege and responsibility to decide and to act over against other persons.[5]

Obedience is a response to authority. In the Bible "obedience," too, has very positive connotations. It is a highly personal concept. To obey is, first of all, *to hear*—that is its root meaning both in Hebrew and in Greek. Obedience occurs when one being listens to another. It is a product of communication. In obeying, a person is not responding primarily to a set of rules or to an abstraction, but to a living person. Furthermore, very basic to the concept of obedience is the element of freedom. Obedience, at least as God's people are to render it, is not the result of coercion, but the willing choice of the believing and loving heart. Although it is acceptance of the will of another, obedience does not involve the destruction of one's own will or the abdication of responsibility. Rather it is the free and responsible decision to comply with the other's will. As such it is not the annihilation of the self, but the voluntary giving of the self in sacrificial service. From the Christian point of view, this is self-fulfillment of the highest order.

Since all legitimate authority is ultimately from God all obedience for the Christian is, ultimately, to be a response to God. The extent to which Scripture and the Lutheran Confessions esteem and elevate the concept of obedience can be seen in the fact the redemptive work of Jesus Christ is frequently described as obedience, obedience to the Father even unto death. The same term is also used, furthermore, to describe the fundamental responses of the Christian to that redemptive work. Both faith and good works are called obedience. In summary, obedience is the free and willing acceptance of and deference to the will of another.[6]

With these rather general definitions in mind, we now turn to the specific concern of this book—authority and obedience in the church. In the context of the current controversy Lutheran educators and others are struggling with numerous serious and difficult questions about authority and obedience and are also expected to assist others in dealing with them. Must I obey the leaders and assemblies of my church? What are the extent and the limitations of their authority and my obligation to obey? Do the leaders or assemblies of the church have a right to insist that I abide by their decisions and comply with their regulations? Does any unit of the church—pastor, teacher, congregation, synod—have the right to tell me what to believe, teach, or do? What freedom or responsibility do I (or my congregation or district) have to make up my (our) own mind(s), evaluate, disagree with, dissent from the resolutions or pronouncements of church assemblies or leaders? Is it loving and just for a majority in the church to impose its will upon a minority? How important is it that we agree in doctrine and practice? To what extent and by what means should we strive for consensus? Do church leaders and assemblies function with God's own authority or only with some form of human authority? And, perhaps, the most basic questions of all: what *is* the authority of the church? Who in the church rightly possesses and exercises it?[7]

Not all of these questions are discussed directly and extensively either in Scripture or the Lutheran Confessions. Patterns of church organization and leadership have changed. For example, democratic forms of church government, as we know them did not exist in those earlier eras. Furthermore, there was not nearly the amount of theological and ecclesiastical diversity then, that we confront today. World views and values are no longer the same. And yet, if we study carefully what Scripture and the Confessions teach about authority and obedience in the church we can, I believe, arrive at a reasonably clear and complete grasp both of the theological concepts and of their application to the present.

In the chapters that follow I summarize the biblical and confessional material under four headings: evangelical authority, confessional authority, disciplinary authority and organizational authority. In reality, these are not four separate and distinct types, but rather different forms or aspects of the one and only authority which the church possesses and is to exercise. The four are, therefore, closely related and the presentation emphasizes this relationship. The appropriate response to each form of authority is obedience. The nature of that obedience, however, varies somewhat from form to form, although each is essentially an expression of the same two-directional love: for God and for people.[8]

A brief comment about each kind of authority will provide the reader with an overview of the contents of the book.

Evangelical authority is the privilege and responsibility to proclaim the Gospel. This is the heart of the matter. The other kinds of authority are merely extensions and applications of this one. Obedience to this authority consists of faith, holiness of life (love), and respect for those who serve as spokesmen of the Gospel.

Confessional authority is the privilege and responsibility to proclaim the Gospel over against current heresy, to clarify and reaffirm the truth of the Gospel in reply to false and inadequate alternatives that are being proposed. Evangelical and organizational authority come together in this process as Christians make collective judgments about truth and error and express their common convictions. Obedience to confessional authority consists of participation in this process and either in accepting or rejecting the product, and, in the case of the latter, making a different confession.

Disciplinary authority is the privilege and responsibility to help those who distort and reject the Gospel (false teachers and impenitent sinners), to correct and restore them if possible, but to exclude them if necessary. The purpose is not to attain or maintain a pure church (this is impossible), but rather to minister to those who are radically disobedient. Obedience to disciplinary authority consists of disassociating with the excluded persons until and unless they repent. In the case of excluded persons obedience would consist of contrition, faith, and correction of life or teaching.

Organizational authority is the privilege and responsibility to organize for the task of proclaiming the Gospel—to form congregations, appoint leaders, establish procedures for worship and work. Obedience to this authority consists of loving cooperation with fellow Christians and faithfulness to agreements.

Even a very brief and preliminary consideration of these categories suggests that most of the disagreements in the Missouri Synod, for example, center in the last three. Some feel that a growing emphasis on disciplinary and organizational authority is a threat to the Gospel, and they feel compelled to confess against this. Others contend that the responsible exercise of evangelical authority requires adequate attention to, and the firm exercise of, the other three as well. The chapters that follow address themselves to these and related issues.

NOTES TO CHAPTER I

[1] Edmund Schlink, *Theology of the Lutheran Confessions*, translated by Paul F. Koehneke and Herbert J. A. Bouman (Philadelphia: Fortress Press, c. 1961), Ch. VI, pp. 194-225. This is an excellent summary interpretation of the confessional material on the doctrine of the church. It directs the reader to the most important sections of the Confessions which deal with this doctrine: Augsburg Confession (A.C.) VII and VIII and the corresponding articles in the Apology of the Augsburg Confession (Ap.), as well as to the discussion of the Third Article of the Creed in Luther's Large Catechism (L.C.). Useful analyses of the

biblical concept of the church are Ph. H. Menoud, "Church," in *A Companion to the Bible*, J. J. Von Allman, ed. (New York: Oxford University Press, 1958) pp. 50-55 and R. H. Fuller, "Church, Assembly," in *A Theological Wordbook of the Bible*. Alan Richardson, ed. (New York: The Macmillan Company, 1951) pp. 46-49.

[2] A classical and definitive Missouri Synod discussion of these aspects of the doctrine of the church is C. F. W. Walther, *Die Stimme unserer Kirche in der Frage von Kirche und Amt*, translated in *Walther and the Church*, by Wm. Dallmann, W. H. T. Dau, and Th. Engelder, editor (Saint Louis: Concordia Publishing House, 1938) pp. 47-86.

[3] *Obedience to Authority: an Experimental View* (New York: Harper and Row, Publishers, c. 1974).

[4] Waldemar Molinski, "Authority," in *Sacramentum Mundi: An Encyclopedia of Theology*, edited by Karl Rahner, *et alii* (New York: Herder and Herder) Vol. 1, p. 129.

[5] Rom. 13:1-7; Eph. 6:1-9; Tit. 3:1-2; 1 Pet. 2:13-3:16. See also Luther's discussion of the Fourth Commandment in the Large Catechism. The article on ἐξουσία in *Theological Dictionary of the New Testament*, edited by Gerhard Kittel, Geoffrey W. Bromily translator and editor (Grand Rapids, Mich.: Wm. B. Erdmans Publishing Company, c. 1964) Vol II pp. 562-575 deals with the New Testament concept of authority.

[6] Articles on ὑπακούειν, ὑποτάσσειν, and πειθεῖν in *ibid.*, review the New Testament concept of obedience. See also references in n. 5 above. Waldemar Molinski's article on "Obedience" in *Sacramentum Mundi,* Vol. 4, pp. 237-241 is a helpful statement from a Roman Catholic perspective.

[7] An interesting series of articles by various authors was published in the *American Lutheran* magazine in 1961 and 1962 on the subject of authority in the church in which these and related questions are explored. Thomas Coates, *Authority in the Church* (Saint Louis: Concordia Publishing House, c. 1964) focuses on similar concerns. These are cited as evidence that a growing preoccupation with authority and obedience in the church surfaced at least a decade before the current controversy.

[8] These terms and categories as such are not found either in Scripture or the Lutheran Confessions. Nor are they used elsewhere in theological literature, to my knowledge. I have coined them as a convenient analytical and conceptual aid. Hopefully, their validity will be established in the chapters that follow.

evangelical
AUTHORITY

Chapter II

Evangelical Authority

The supreme authority of the church, the highest privilege and most important responsibility bestowed upon Christians is that of proclaiming the Gospel. Every other form of authority in the church is to be expressive of the Gospel or in the service of the Gospel. The church is created by the Gospel and exists primarily for the purpose of communicating that Gospel. This central and dominant authority — to proclaim the Gospel — is referred to in this book as "evangelical authority." ("Evangel" equals "Gospel," or "good news.")

At first glance this might appear to be authority of a very low order, perhaps no real authority at all. We tend to think of authority primarily in terms of controlling people and confining people. That person appears to have real authority who can tell others what to do and enforce his will upon them. Authority is the power to hire and to fire, to regulate and to legislate. However, the basic authority of the church has a decidedly different character and purpose. It is the authority to liberate, to heal, to restore (Matt. 10:1; 16:13-20; Jn. 20:21-23). Those who exercise this evangelical authority rescue and elevate others. They do not box them in or hold them down. They render a loving and humble service. They do not abuse or demean. The church is authorized and empowered by its Lord to function in these ways, to be His herald and agent of salvation. We perceive our authority in the church most clearly and exercise it most faithfully when we conform to this model. Perhaps one of the most serious problems that we experience as we discuss or employ authority in the church is the tendency to lose sight of this redemptive and supportive model of authority and revert to a domineering and even punitive model.

Jesus is the Authority

The authority of the church in all its forms is, essentially, Jesus Christ Himself. It is a person rather than a thing or an abstraction. Jesus' authority is both personal and official. He possesses it not only by virtue of who He is but also by virtue of what He has done and can do. The New Testament pictures the historical Jesus as a person who had great authority. He spoke and acted for God, made God known to people, counteracted the evil forces that hold human beings in misery and sin. His hearers noted that He taught with authority and not as their scribes (Mk. 1:22). He wielded authority over demons (Mk. 1:28). He claimed and demonstrated power both to forgive and to heal (Mk. 2:1-12). Just prior to His ascension He announced that all authority in heaven and on earth had been given to Him (Matt. 28:18). Now, at the right hand of God, He is above all other rule and authority, is head over all things (Eph. 1:20-23; Col. 1:17-18). He is the head and Lord of the church which is His body (Eph. 5:23). He functions in and through the church.

Jesus is the Gospel. The authority to proclaim the Gospel is the privilege and responsibility of bearing witness to Jesus Christ. All of God's love and help are wrapped up in Him. Pardon, deliverance from evil of every kind, power to become new people, and the promise of eternal life are all based on what Jesus was, did, and endured in this world.[1] No one can be put in touch with these blessings except through exposure to Jesus.[2] God is saying something to us human beings through Jesus, and it is very good news. He is saying that He loves us despite our sin, and that He has identified with us. He is saying that by a terrible ordeal of self-sacrifice He has atoned for our sin (Rom. 5:6-10). He is saying that through faith in Jesus we can belong to Him and to one another forever (1 Jn. 1). He is saying that already in this life we can begin to break the tyranny of sin and experience transformation into His likeness (2 Cor. 3:17-4:6).

To equate the Gospel with Jesus is completely consistent with both Scripture and the Lutheran Confessions. The Gospel that Jesus preached and which He commanded the Twelve and the Seventy to preach prior to His death and resurrection was the Gospel of the Kingdom of God (Mk. 1:15; Matt. 10:7ff; Lk. 10:4), that God's redemptive and restorative rule was present and active among them in a new and decisive way. However, all this had a very close and personal connection with Jesus Himself. "The kingdom of God is at hand," means, "I, your divine King, am here to rescue you from the dark powers which possess and torment you, and to bring you under my own pardon, protection, and influence." After Christ's glorification, i.e., His resurrection and ascension, the Gospel is defined more specifically as the "Gospel of Christ" (Rom. 1:16; 15:

19; 1 Cor. 9:12, 18), meaning not only the Gospel which Christ preached but also the Gospel which has Christ as its content.

In the Confessions the Gospel is defined, in its narrow sense as the consoling promise of the forgiveness of sins[3] or justification by grace for Christ's sake through faith.[4] This is not understood, however, in an abstract or impersonal sense, but as the offer of Christ Himself: ". . . for the Gospel shows us Christ and promises the forgiveness of sins freely for his sake. . . This promise bids us trust that because of Christ we are reconciled to the Father. . . ."[5] The Gospel in the Confessions is never simply a juridical transaction ("Sinner, your case is dismissed!"). Rather, it is that which communicates Jesus Christ and all that He has done in a highly personal manner ("Sinner, Jesus offers you Himself and all that He has done!").

Authority Given to the Apostles

The authority to proclaim the Gospel was transmitted to the church beginning with the apostles. Already during His earthly ministry but especially between His resurrection and ascension Jesus commanded and empowered them to do this. They were to be His witnesses (Matt. 10:1-23; Lk. 24:44-49; Acts 1:8). They were to make disciples of all nations (Matt. 28:19). In other words, they were to present to others the Jesus whom they knew and trusted. They were to tell others what they had heard from Him and seen Him do and suffer. They were to invite and encourage them also to accept His offer of rescue and to become His followers. The apostles were specifically authorized to represent Jesus, to speak and act for Him in this way. And, especially after the empowering experience of Pentecost, they exercised this authority with great confidence and effect. The Book of Acts is the record of evangelical authority at work in the apostolic church. Through their preaching of Jesus' death and resurrection and through Baptism they forgave sins and united people to Him and to one another (Acts 2; 5:12-16). This was always the primary emphasis of their ministries, their chief concern — to proclaim the Gospel of forgiveness.

There were also other ways in which they represented Jesus Christ and functioned for Him in the world. In His name they healed the sick and the infirm (Acts 3:1-9; 9:32-35), expelled demons (Acts 8:7; 16:8), and even raised the dead (Acts 9:36-43; 20:7-12). While no miraculous feedings are reported, comparable to Jesus' extension of the loaves and fishes, the apostles did lead the early Christians in an extensive and generous ministry to material needs (Acts 2:44-46; 4:32; 6:1-6). Like Jesus, they taught the Word of God and celebrated the eucharist, fostered the fellowship of believers, and led them in prayer (Acts 2:42; 4:23-31). Furthermore, in a Christlike manner they identified and condemned impenitence (Acts 5:1-11) and false doctrine (Acts 15:1-29) and corrected those who erred ignorantly (Acts 19:1-7). In short, the apostles, under the charge and by the power of Jesus Christ, said and did the sorts of things in this world that characterized His own earthly life and ministry.

Authority to Proclaim the Gospel in its Fulness

The evangelical authority possessed and exercised by the apostles was comprehensive. At its heart and center was the word of forgiveness, but growing out of this was a rich and diverse application. Evangelical authority should not be perceived too narrowly. It is the task of communicating the Gospel in its fulness. In addition to the elements already mentioned, several others must be added if the concept of evangelical authority is to be complete.

1. *Proclamation of the Law*

In the first place, the authority to proclaim the Gospel also includes the responsibility to proclaim the law. In its broad sense the word "Gospel" includes law and is frequently used this way both in Scripture and in the Confessions. To be effective the Gospel must be presented in conjunction with the law. Law and Gospel must be distinguished, but never separated. They are very different. The law speaks of God's demands upon us and His anger and judgment upon our failure to comply. The Gospel speaks of God's love and gift of pardon in Jesus Christ. The law frightens and kills. The Gospel consoles and makes alive. They are antithetical, opposites.

In its narrow sense, when set over against the law, "Gospel" means only the message of God's mercy for the sake of Christ. In its broader sense it means the total proclamation, including both law and Gospel.[6] Law and Gospel function in both a dialectical and a complementary manner. One will not work effectively without the other. The solution which the Gospel offers seems irrelevant to the person who has not been made aware of his or her problem by the law. The cure of the Gospel is unwelcome unless a person has received the shattering diagnosis of the law.

Conversely, apart from the Gospel the law can not help a person or even be fully understood. Apart from the offer of a solution and a cure, awareness of the problem and the disease of sin can only demoralize or stimulate false hope. In fact, apart from the Gospel, neither the character of the law nor its purpose can be adequately known.

The relation between law and Gospel in the Christian message, and in the Christian life, is not that of an equal partnership. One of the elements is and must remain supreme – the Gospel. The law must be proclaimed in the interest of the Gospel and not *vice versa.* The bad news of the law is announced in order to prepare a person for the good news of the Gospel. It is just the opposite of the relationship between good and bad news in the jokes that have been making the rounds in recent years. In these, the good news is always stated first in order to set someone up for the bad news. In these jokes the bad news is always the punch-line. In the Christian message the bad news of the law sets the hearer up for the good news of the Gospel. In this case the good news is the punch-line. And yet, unless the law has done its preparatory work, the punch-line of the Gospel will not register. Evangelical authority, the privilege and responsibility to proclaim the Gospel, involves proclaiming the Gospel in its fulness, in its broad sense, and that means law as well as Gospel.[7]

2. *God's Entire Self-Disclosure*

The proper exercise of evangelical authority, furthermore, includes the communication of God's entire self-disclosure in Christ and in Scripture. The heart and core of this authority is the proclamation of law and Gospel, but extending outward from this center is the broader privilege and responsibility to proclaim God's entire revelation. The expansion of evangelical authority in this manner can be traced in the sequence of events recorded in the Gospels. Late in His ministry, in a very direct and explicit manner Jesus gave this central core authority to bind and loose sins first to Peter (Matt. 16:19-20), and then to the other disciples (Matt. 18:18). In the Upper Room on the night before His death Jesus promised His disciples that the Holy Spirit would come to them, teach them all things, and enable them to remember *all* that He had said (Jn. 14: 26). The Holy Spirit would guide them into *all* truth, clarify, confirm, apply and extend the revelation which had been given to them through Jesus Christ (Jn. 16:12-15). Then, after His resurrection on the evening of Easter day He reaffirmed their authority to proclaim the Gospel (Jn. 20:22-23). On that same occasion He enabled them to see and understand how the Old Testament Scriptures bore witness to Him. He charged them to proclaim repentance and forgiveness of sins through His suffering and death on the basis of those Scriptures as well as on the basis of their own experiences and observations.[8] In the Great Commission shortly before His ascension Jesus commanded them to teach others to observe *all* that He had commanded them (Matt. 28:20).

From this it is clear that the basic authority granted by Christ to the apostles included the privilege and responsibility of sharing God's total manifestation of Himself: the written word of the Old Testament as well as the Incarnate Word Jesus. Furthermore, it included the authority and the resources with which ultimately to produce the New Testament Scriptures. Evangelical authority involves witness to the Gospel in its fulness. It must be understood broadly.

The Gospel is not merely one doctrine of Scripture, even the most important doctrine. Nor is it merely one series of episodes in Scripture, even the most important episodes. Rather, the Gospel is the unifying theme which permeates and explicates all scriptural doctrines and events. All Scripture bears witness to Christ (Jn. 5:39). All that Christ is and does supports, unfolds, or applies the scriptural Gospel of forgiveness. The Gospel is the summary of Scripture, the expression of its very essence, and Scripture is the divinely inspired and authoritative source of the Gospel.[9] As they taught in the Old Testament Scriptures and eventually wrote the New Testament Scriptures, the apostles were exercising evangelical authority. They were proclaiming the Gospel in its fulness. In order to carry out our responsibility to the Gospel today we must communicate the entire biblical testimony, in the light of the Gospel.

3. *Implications for the Christian Life*

Still another aspect of evangelical authority is teaching the implications of the Gospel for the Christian life. A significant portion of Jesus' own teaching and preaching ministry was devoted to moral instruction. Not only in the Sermon on the Mount (Matt. 5-7), but also in His parables (Matt. 18:23-25; Lk. 10:25-37; 15:17-32; 18:9-14; etc.) and other discourses[10] Jesus gives careful attention to the value and behavioral changes which should and will characterize those who believe the Gospel. In this aspect of His teaching Jesus was prescriptive as well as descriptive. In a forthright and authoritative manner He told His followers what they should do and what they should avoid, what was right and what was wrong.

The apostolic writings reveal a similar emphasis on moral direction. Paul,[11] Peter (1 Pet. 2-5), John,[12] and James in his epistle present as part of their Gospel proclamation, imperatives and models for Christian living. It is important to distinguish between these moral imperatives addressed to Christians and the demands of God's law. In some respects they are similar. The New Testament moral imperatives, like the law, are from God. Both express His will for human conduct. Both are given in the form of "do" and "don't" statements. And yet, there is also a significant difference. The commandments of the law are addressed primarily to the human being as sinner and are designed to expose and condemn sin, to reveal God's wrath for sin. Christian moral instruction is addressed to people who are forgiven through faith in Jesus Christ. It is based on the Gospel and the relation to the Gospel is always evident, implicitly if not explicitly. It tells believers the kind of new people they can and should become because God forgives their sins and equips them with the enabling power of His Holy Spirit. Christian moral imperatives may properly be called "Gospel imperatives" because they are part of the Gospel message, rather than the law. They are related to, and expressive of, God's gift of love in Jesus Christ. They tell us not only what we must do but what we can do through God's gift of Christ and the Spirit. The Gospel in its fulness says not only, "Your sins are forgiven for Jesus' sake," but also, "With His love and Spirit He will enable you to struggle against sin and to grow into His own likeness."[13]

In this connection it is important to note that justification and sanctification, although they must be distinguished, must never be separated. Both are gifts of God and essential components of the Gospel. It is an error to identify only justification with the Gospel and to associate sanctification with the law. "Through God's grace you can change (and, therefore should)" is as much a part of the Good News as "God does not hold your sins against you."

In the witness to the Gospel, justification does have primacy. God's forgiveness in Christ is the basis of His transforming work in the believer. Because He pardons us He also changes us, but not *vice versa*. Sanctification is a result of justification. That does not mean, however, that sanctification is optional or dispensible. It is a necessary result of justification and an integral part of the Gospel.[14] It is not legalism to teach God's revealed will for the Christian life even in a very specific manner in terms of detailed and binding directives. Rather, when properly done, this is part of the proclamation of the Gospel. If Christian moral instruction is isolated from the Gospel, or if sanctification is presented as the grounds for justification, then the presentation has deteriorated into either legalism or moralism. If the imperatives are presented as new possibilities which are part of God's gracious work in the believer, that is a valid and necessary exercise of evangelical authority. One of the many possible examples of this from the New Testament itself is: "Beloved, let us love one another" (1 Jn. 4:7). This is an imperative, something we are told to do. Notice, however, the Gospel affirmations and promises connected with it which describe the doing of this as God's own gift and work: ". . . he who loves is born of God and knows God" (1 Jn. 4:7). "In this the love of God was manifest among us, that God sent his only Son into the world that we might live through him" (1 Jn. 4:9).

Authority Supported and Implemented by the Spirit

1. *The Promise of the Spirit*

In order to prepare and equip His apostles to proclaim the Gospel in its fulness, to exercise evangelical authority, Jesus Christ sent them His Holy Spirit. He had promised them the Spirit. On Holy Thursday, He had explained His role in their ministries during the Upper Room discourses preserved for us in the Gospel of John. Jesus was about to go away, not only in the sense that He would be killed, but also in the sense that after the resurrection His visible presence would be withdrawn. In His absence they would have a great work to do in His name and in His place. They would not have to undertake this task alone, however, or on their own resources. Someone else, the Spirit, would come to be with them and to help them. He would counsel and inform them. He would aid their recollection and understanding so that they could faithfully and effectively communicate His saving word and work to the world (Jn. 14).

The opposition would be severe. By persecution and death the world would try to stop them. The Spirit would support and sustain them, however. He would also accompany their message of law and Gospel and work in the hearts of their hearers through it. In all that He would do in and through them, the Holy Spirit would not be functioning independently. He would represent Christ and reveal Christ, and, through Christ, the Father as well (Jn. 15:18-16:15).

2. *Fulfillment of the Promise*

What Christ promised in the Upper Room He delivered dramatically after His resurrection. Already on Easter evening, in a quiet and preliminary manner, He breathed the enabling power of the Holy Spirit into them (Jn. 20:22). However, the full and explosive outpouring came about seven weeks later on Pentecost. The apostles, in fact, all of the believers present, were filled with the Holy Spirit. Immediately, they launched into a bold and effective witnessing campaign in which they were able, temporarily at least, to preach in languages which they had never learned (Acts 2:4-12). He gave them courage to speak fearlessly to the very council which had plotted Jesus' death (Acts 4:8, 38). The Holy Spirit directed them in their missionary planning (Acts 13:2, 4; 16:6) and even in their individual witnessing contacts (Acts 8:29). He witnessed to and through them (Acts 5:32). The Spirit sustained them during persecution (Acts 7:55), gave them some sense of what to expect in the future (Acts 20:23, 28), guided their collective doctrinal decisions (Acts 15:28), and, in general, blessed them with serenity and success (Acts 9:30).

Furthermore, through the apostolic witness and ministry the Holy Spirit was transmitted to others (Acts 2:38; 10:44; 11:5; 19:6). Commenting on the relation of the Holy Spirit to his own Gospel ministry, St. Paul says:

> We have received not the spirit of the world, but the Spirit which is from God, that we might understand the gifts bewtowed on us by God. And we impart this in words not taught by human wisdom but taught by the Spirit. . . (1 Cor. 2:12-13).

Not only the perception but also the communication of the Gospel, written as well as spoken, was influenced and controlled by the Spirit. Elsewhere St. Paul makes a similar claim, "Our Gospel came to you not only in word but also in power and in the Holy Spirit and with full conviction" (1 Thess. 1:5). St. Peter refers to himself and the other apostolic witnesses as "those who preached the good news to you through the Holy Spirit sent from heaven" (1 Pet. 1:12). St. John explains that, ultimately, the chief witness to Jesus who functioned through the instrumentality of the apostles was the Holy Spirit Himself (1 Jn. 5:6). Eventually, it was through the inspiration and direction of the Holy Spirit that the apostles and their associates were able to produce the New Testament Scriptures and thus to preserve the Gospel in its fulness in written form. In a unique and complete manner the apostles' exercise of evangelical authority, their proclamation of the Gospel, was supported and implemented by the Holy Spirit.

However, the Holy Spirit also supports and implements the exercise of evangelical authority today. Not only the apostolic witnesses but all who communicate the Gospel have the benefit of His presence and influence. With regard to Scripture this means that not only those who originally wrote the biblical documents were inspired, but, in a certain sense, also those who teach and preach Christ on the basis of these documents. The concept of inspiration goes even beyond this. The hearers and readers of the Scriptural message are also inspired. The same Holy Spirit who moved the authors to write as they did, now, through these words, reaches and influences all who receive them. Through the Word and sacraments, and only through the Word and sacraments, is the Holy Spirit given. We who exercise evangelical authority today by teaching and preaching the Gospel in its fulness have the assurance that a great power and authority is working through that Word, the power of the Holy Spirit to convert, strengthen, and console.[15]

Authority to be Exercised by All Christ's People

The privilege and responsibility of proclaiming the Gospel in the New Testament age was not confined to the apostles. From the very beginning it belonged to all believers and was exercised by all. On Pentecost, not only the Twelve but the entire assembly of believers received the outpouring of the Holy Spirit and proclaimed the mighty works of God in Jesus Christ (Acts 2:1-11). At least two of the seven men who were chosen to administer the material aid program of the Jerusalem congregation soon became conspicuous also for their public witness to Christ—Stephen (Acts 6:8-7:60) and

Philip (Acts 8:4-40). After Saul initiated the persecution of Christians in Jerusalem, many believers fled to various locations throughout Judea and Samaria. Wherever they went, these ordinary believers went about preaching the Gospel word (Acts 8:1-4).

Writing to the Christians in Asia Minor St. Peter reminds them that they are a chosen race, a royal priesthood, a holy nation, God's own people who are to declare His wonderful deeds in Christ and are always to be prepared to bear witness to their Lord and the hope they have in Him (1 Pet. 2:9, 3:15). According to St. Paul, the church is the body of Christ, and all members are gifted by the Spirit both for faith and for service. The gifts differ. Some are more intellectual and verbal. Others are more affective and active. But all are centered in the purpose of communicating and demonstrating the Gospel (Rom. 12:1-8; 1 Cor. 12:1-11, 27-31). Not only the apostles but all the saints are to be equipped for the work of the ministry. That work consists of building up the body of Christ both by adding new members and by strengthening those who already belong. The process by which the body is built up is the proclaiming and living of the Gospel, "speaking the truth in love" (Eph. 4:1-16). All Christians, then, possess evangelical authority.

In order to equip and train His people to exercise this authority Christ has given them leaders. The role of the leaders in relation to the members is clearly defined. They do not possess and exercise this authority for the members. Rather, they help the members to use this authority themselves, faithfully and effectively. Church leaders not only dispense God's Word of grace to and for the members. They also educate and motivate members to dispense that Word to one another and to the world. The role of a church leader is comparable to that of a playing-coach who gives instruction and direction, not from the sidelines, but from the midst of the contest, not only by words and diagrams, but by his or her own participation and example.

Such a support system is mutual. Leaders are themselves built up by the members whom they serve (Eph. 4:10-16; Rom. 1:10-11; Phil 1:3-7). Those who function in these leadership roles and offices are not simply volunteers or human appointees, but the gifts and representatives of God (Jn. 15:16, 20:21; Acts 20:28; Rom. 12: 6-8; 1 Cor. 12:28; Eph. 4:11; 2 Tim. 1:11, 14; etc.).

A considerable amount of variety is evident in the leadership of the church already in the New Testament era. Apostles and their seven "social worker" assistants have been mentioned. Elders are referred to both in the Jewish congregation in Jerusalem (Acts 11: 30, 15:2, etc.), and in the Gentile congregations outside Palestine (Acts 14:23, 20:17; 2 Tim. 5:1, 17; Titus 1:5; 1 Pet. 5:1; etc.). Bishops (overseers) are also referred to in several places (Phil. 1:1; 1 Tim. 3:1-13). Other terms used for church leaders are prophets, teachers, evangelists, pastors, etc. (1 Cor. 12:28; Eph. 4:11). The precise function of each and the relation of these functions and offices to each other is not always easy to determine. It is clear, however, that they were complementary ministries devoted to the communication of the Gospel and its implications. They were designed to equip, nurture, and lead the believers in their exercise of evangelical authority and in their role as Gospel proclaimers. To this end they instructed, admonished, guided and guarded the church, both in doctrine and in Christian living. The positive presentation of Christ and the life that He calls His people to lead was combined with warning against and rejection of everyone and everything that contradicted this.[16]

Other ministries are a continuation and extension of the apostolic ministries. Although there were differences between the apostles and other New Testament leaders the authority was essentially the same, that of proclaiming the Gospel. The apostles were unique in that Jesus called them to their work personally and directly (Matt. 5:17-22, 9:9; Jn. 1:35-49; etc.). Other leaders were selected by an assembly of believers (Acts 6:1-6), or appointed by the apostles (Acts 14:23), or even by their associates (Tit. 1:5). In addition, the apostles (except for Paul) had been intimate associates of Jesus and personal observers of His saving works (Lk. 24:48; Jn. 15:27), while other leaders received their information and interpretation through the apostles and other witnesses (Acts 20:27-35; 2 Tim. 1:3-14). The apostles, furthermore, enjoyed unique gifts of the Spirit, enabling them to recall, retell, and record the Gospel revelation in a precise and authoritative manner (Jn. 14:25-26, 16:12-15; 1 Cor. 2:12-13; 1 Pet. 1:12). Every other ministry is derived from and dependent upon the apostolic ministries. In order to carry out the Risen Lord's charge to make disciples of all nations the apostles had to enlist and train others to perpetuate and multiply their witness. These leaders had exactly the same authority as the apostles—to forgive sins, to share the good news of Christ. The apostles treated other leaders as colleagues, not as subordinates (1 Pet. 5:1; 2 Jn. 1; 3 Jn. 1; Col. 4:7; Phil. 2:25). The apostles referred to their new colleagues also as called by God into their offices (Acts 20:28) and described them as the gifts of God to His church (1 Cor. 12:28; Eph. 4:11).[17]

Evangelical authority is to be exercised by all of Christ's people, and that includes His people today. Not only the apostles and their colleagues in church leadership roles, not only the total membership of the New Testament church, but all of Christ's people in every age have the privilege and responsibility to proclaim the Gospel. What is the authority that *we* have as we serve in the classroom, in the pulpit, and at the desk? What is the authority that we have as Christian congregations and groups of congregations? What is the authority that we have as Christian individuals in this late Twentieth Century? The answer for us is precisely the same as it was for those New Testament Christians and their leaders.

Our basic and supreme authority is the right and the duty to announce to people that Christ has obtained pardon for them and the possibility of new personhood. Our chief purpose in this world individually and collectively is the communication of this great news. Like the New Testament leaders, we who hold offices of leadership in the church today have as our primary function to assist and encourage the members to speak and to live the Gospel more effectively. How do we accomplish this? By bringing that Gospel to them, along with its sacramental enactments, at every possibility and in every appropriate way. We teach and preach the Word and administer Baptism and the Lord's Supper so that people might believe in Christ, belong to Him, grow in Him, and share Him with one another and the world. Everything that we do in the church, every program, every learning situation, every worship service, every office, every decision, every fund, every institution, every appointment, every assembly, directly or indirectly is to serve this purpose. It is to be an exercise of evangelical authority, an expression of the Gospel.

As we spell out the relevance to the present, the witness of the Lutheran Confessions is particularly helpful. As the Confessors struggled with questions and problems of church authority in their day, as they worked out the implications of the New Testament teaching for their situation, they provided us with a model and perspective for understanding church authority today.

What in this book we call "evangelical authority" the Confessors include in the terms "spiritual authority," or "spiritual power," or the "power of the keys," or the "power of bishops." It is the task of preaching the Gospel and administering the sacraments, of forgiving and retaining sins.[18] This authority is a function to carry out rather than an official position to fill.[19] It is a work, a job, which Christ has given His people to do, rather than a special caste which He has established. This assignment and authorization has been given to *all* people, not just to a select group of leaders. The power can be fully operational in any group of believers and even in a Christian individual.[20]

The Confessors also acknowledge the validity and necessity of a public ministry, of designated individuals who will lead the assembled Christians in the exercise of this authority, who will teach and preach the Gospel and administer the sacraments in their midst.[21] Christ Himself, through the calling of the apostles, instituted these leadership roles.[22] A person in a public ministry is not simply an appointee of a congregation functioning with authority delegated by the members. He is also the agent and representative of Jesus Christ. People are called into ministries by Christ through the selection and recognition procedures of the church. In designating persons for public Gospel ministries, God's people act not independently, but in the name and at the command of their Lord.[23] When calling people into ministries, the believers do not delegate or transfer their spiritual authority to them. Instead, they exercise their authority and fulfill their Gospel function through these leaders. The relation between the spiritual leaders and the congregation is reciprocal rather than one in which either party dominates. The church does its public preaching by calling individuals into the ministry of teaching and preaching the Gospel, and the church is built up when these called individuals do their teaching and preaching. The over-riding emphasis in the entire discussion of spiritual authority is that ultimately the authority is the Lord Himself who rules both congregation and leaders through the Gospel and Sacraments.[24]

If we compare this summary of confessional teaching about spiritual authority with the summary of New Testament teaching given above, we note a somewhat different emphasis. The Confessions do

not appear to say as much as the New Testament does about the equipping and implementing role of church leaders, or indicate that their goal is to prepare and assist the members in their proclamation of the Gospel. The emphasis in the Confessions appears to be on the members' functioning through their leaders, proclaiming the Gospel through these spokespersons. This is not an error on the part of the Confessors. Nowhere do they deny that church leaders are to train their members for witness. In fact, such training is clearly implied. The difference in emphasis can be accounted for by the somewhat different purposes which each set of writers was trying to accomplish.

The New Testament writers were primarily trying to raise the consciousness of new Christians regarding their potential and their unity. Prior to their conversion they were aliens and outcasts from God and at odds with one another, trapped in futility and sin.Now they are reconciled to God and to one another. They are endowed with the resources of God's own Spirit, and they have vital contributions to make to one another and to the world. Believers are to communicate His truth, make known His glory, bring light into the darkness of the world. They are to help one another to function in this way, and their leaders can be of special assistance.[25]

The confessional writers, on the other hand, while in full agreement with all of this, also have some specifically polemical purposes in mind. They are writing against the medieval Roman view that only the clergy possess spiritual authority and that only the bishops can transmit this authority by ordaining new clergy. In reply to this the Confessors affirm that the whole church, all members, possess spiritual authority and, therefore, the right to ordain clergy. They insist that the clergy function for, and not only over against, the laity. However, the Confessors do not pursue extensively the priestly role of the laity in their daily lives or their preparation for this by the clergy. They simply did not carry the discussion this far.[26]

Not the Authority to Coerce

Both Scripture and the Confessions specifically reject the notion that the authority of the church includes the right to accomplish its purposes by force, or that this authority may properly be combined with coercion. The authority of the church is evangelical authority. It is the right and the duty to announce good news, not the right and the duty to compel. Jesus forbade His disciples to lord it over one another. Instead, He urged them to accept the humble servant role (Matt. 20:25, 26; 23:8-12). Peter admonished elders not to domineer over their flocks, but to be an example (1 Pet. 5: 1-3). In His dealings with congregations and with Christian individuals, Paul consistently refused to make demands or to pull spiritual rank on the basis of His apostolic office. Instead he chose to plead, to persuade, to encourage people to do what he directed in response to the Gospel.[27]

The Confessions also dwell upon this matter extensively. The authority of bishops is described in broad terms which cover most of the categories discussed in this book. It is the authority to preach the Gospel, to forgive sins (what we are calling "evangelical authority"), to evaluate doctrine and reject whatever is false (our term for this is "confessional authority"), and to exclude manifest and impenitent sinners ("disciplinary authority" is our phrase). Then an important qualification is added: "All this is to be done *not by human power*, but by God's Word alone."[28] (Emphasis added.) It was necessary to denounce the use of human power because many bishops of that time were temporal rulers as well as ecclesiastical leaders. As such, they had a considerable amount of clout.[29] They could use the threat of imprisonment or even the death penalty to enforce compliance with their church teaching and regulation. Or, if they did not possess temporal authority themselves, they frequently secured the cooperation of those who did in order to assure conformity with their official demands.[30]

Replying to Lutheran criticism on these points, the Roman opponents insisted that bishops do "have the power to rule and correct by force in order to guide their subjects toward the goal of eternal bliss. . ." Bishops, moreover, claimed as part of their church authority the right to establish and impose new ceremonies and regulations upon the members, which were regarded as binding and necessary to salvation.[31] This the Lutheran Confessors vehemently denounced. Bishops, they said, have the authority to proclaim the Gospel, not to contradict it by human ordinances which they present as meritorious. These Lutherans insisted that Christ's glory is blasphemed by any alternative or additive to His redemptive work. Such ordinances are not binding upon Christians, and to disregard them is not sin. Consciences should not be burdened. Christian liberty must be preserved.[32] That is to say, neither the church as a whole nor its leaders have the authority to change or to supplement scriptural teaching on doctrine or morality. Nor does church authority include the right to secure conformity by external force. The only power by which the church is to function in building Christian faith and prompting Christian obedience is the power of the Word.[33]

Commitment to the sole authority of the Word and renunciation of all coercion in the church was stated eloquently and forcefully by C.F.W. Walther in his presidential address at the 1848 convention of the Missouri Synod. The question which he chose to consider was, "Why Should and Can We Carry On Our Work Joyfully Although We Have No Power but the Power of the Word?" His answer: This is the only power Christ has given to His servants. Even the apostles claimed no other power, and they specifically warned others against claiming any power other than the Word. The only power in the Kingdom of Christ is the Lord Himself, and He exercises it by His Word. Those who lead and rule in the church are to do so by proclaiming the Word and administering the sacraments, which accompany and seal that Word. Those who claim a power in the church beside the Word are robbing the church of Christ of its liberty purchased with the Savior's blood. They are infringing upon His divine Kingship. Where the Word does not regulate, the people of God have the freedom to decide what should be done, and they should not be submitted to coercion by their leaders or anyone else. The Word is the only power at all levels in the church — synodical as well as congregational.[34]

Obedience to Evangelical Authority

Obedience as defined in the previous chapter (p.6) is the acceptance of and deference to the will of another, specifically, a person with some kind of authority. It begins with hearing and more importantly with listening to another. Obedience is the result of personal encounter and communication. If in my relationship with a person of authority I make a free and informed and, therefore, responsible choice to comply with his or her wishes, that is obedience from the Christian perspective. Obedience, then, is a response to authority. The form of the response will be determined in part by the nature of the authority which it confronts. The question before us at this point is: what is obedience to evangelical authority? If we rephrase the question in such a way as to indicate the meaning of the key term ("evangelical authority"), the answer becomes more obvious. To ask how we are to obey evangelical authority is simply to ask how we are to respond to the Gospel.

In the first place, obedience to evangelical authority is *faith in the Gospel.* The response which God hopes for when He confronts us with His love in Christ is that we will accept Him and His love, and count on this above everything else. When the church exercises evangelical authority over against us, or to others through our ministries, it is simply presenting the Gospel. To obey this authority is to believe in Jesus Christ.

Both Scripture and the Confessions describe faith in the Gospel also as obedience. St. Paul speaks of "the obedience of faith" (Rom. 1:5, 16:26), meaning the obedience which is faith, the acceptance of God's gracious will to save. Paul also speaks of those who do or do not "obey the Gospel," and this phrase, too, is a synonym for faith: "But they have not all heeded (literally "obeyed") the Gospel, for Isaiah says, 'Lord who has believed what he has heard from us,'" (Rom. 10:17. Cf. also 2 Thess. 1:8). Another passage which uses the word "obey" in the sense of faith in Jesus is the following: "And being made perfect he (Jesus) became the source of salvation to all who obey him" (Heb. 5:9; cf. also Rom. 15:18; 2 Cor. 10:5; and 1 Pet. 1:2). Still others describe faith as obedience to the truth – the truth of the Gospel (Rom. 2:8; Gal. 5:7; 1 Pet. 1:22). A magnificent interpretation of faith as obedience to the Gospel was formulated by Philip Melanchthon:

> But that virtue justifies which takes hold of Christ, communicating to us Christ's merits and, through them, grace and peace from God. This virtue is faith. As we have often said, faith is not merely knowledge but rather a desire to accept and grasp what is offered in the promise of Christ. *This obedience toward God, this desire to receive the offered promise,* is no less an act of worship than is love. God wants us to believe in him and to accept blessings from him. . .[35] (emphasis added)

According to the Confessions, not only faith, but also the object of faith, the Gospel, is described as obedience. That about Jesus Christ on which we rely for our salvation is His perfect obedience to the demands of God's law and His obedient submission to the condemnation of that law, in our place and for our sake. To believe is to obey (accept) the Gospel, and the Gospel is the message of Christ's obedience for us.[36]

Obedience to the church and in the church is a response to the authority of the church. The living center of that authority is Jesus Christ and God's offer of grace in Him, that is to say, the Gospel. To obey the church is, above all, to obey the Gospel, and that, as we have seen, is to believe in Jesus Christ.

A second aspect of obedience to evangelical authority is *holiness of life*, attitudes and conduct which conform to the will of God. An essential element of the Gospel is the gift of personal transformation by the power of the Holy Spirit, the gift of sanctification. For Christ's sake God not only wants to forgive us, He also wants to change us for the better and He offers this to us in the Good News. To accept the Gospel, then, is to accept both parts of the promise, sanctification as well as justification. We who by faith receive the obedience of Christ which covers our disobedience and makes us acceptable to God, receive with this the power to begin to become obedient ourselves. Obedience to evangelical authority, to the Gospel, is joyfully and gratefully to choose the values and behavior patterns which our Lord prescribes. That is, we try to love Him above all else, and others as ourselves. Motivated by Christ's love, guided and empowered by the Spirit, we willingly accept and try to follow the guidance for life which He gives us in Scripture.

Numerous New Testament references express this aspect of obedience to the Gospel. After describing the manner in which we have been set free from the guilt and bondage of sin by the death and resurrection of Christ, St. Paul goes on to say, ". . . you who once were slaves of sin have become obedient from the heart to the standard of teaching to which you were committed" (Rom. 6:17). St. Peter shows how the response of holiness grows out of one's grasp of the atoning work of Christ:

> As obedient children, do not be conformed to the passions of your former ignorance, but as he who called you is holy, be holy yourselves in all your conduct. You know that you were ransomed from the futile ways inherited from your fathers, not with perishable things such as silver and gold, but with the precious blood of Christ. (1 Peter 1:14, 18-19)

The Confessions also teach that part of obedience to the Gospel is the decision to obey God's will by the power of the Holy Spirit.[37]

Although good works are not to be regarded as a cause of justification, they are a necessary result of justification. Those who are regenerated by the Holy Spirit are obligated to do good works, not by coercion or compulsion of the law, but as a response to the Gospel.[38] The new obedience of the Christian is a gift of God's grace to be accepted by faith and acted out in life.[39]

Finally, obedience to evangelical authority also involves *respect for the spokesmen of the Gospel.* If we respect and cherish the Gospel, we will also highly esteem those through whom God brings the Gospel to us. Not the persons themselves but the Gospel which they proclaim and the Lord whom they represent is the grounds of this respect (Lk. 10:16). We demonstrate our respect for these Gospel-bearers, not by man-worship or by uncritical acceptance of all that they say and do, but by receiving and heeding the Word which they bring (1 Thess. 2:13). Paul, for instance, expresses deep concern about the faltering obedience of the Corinthian Christians over against himself (2 Cor. 2:9, 10:6). He urges them to be subject also to others who have devoted themselves to the service of the saints (1 Cor. 16:16). Moreover, he calls upon Christians to ban any who refuse to accept his apostolic message (2 Thess. 3:14). "Obey your leaders and submit to them, for they are keeping watch over your souls," says the author of Hebrews (13:17). These and similar injunctions require, as a response to the Gospel, a deferential attitude and manner toward the Gospel messengers. Included also is the responsibility to provide for the material needs of these leaders: ". . . the Lord commanded that all those who proclaim the gospel should get their living by the gospel" (1 Cor. 10:14; cf. also 1 Tim. 5:17). Confessional material on this point is not extensive. However, there is a clear directive that ministers and churches obey bishops when they properly exercise their Gospel authority.[40] In addition, there is Luther's charge to honor and provide for "spiritual fathers."[41]

Walther has summarized his vision of obedience to spiritual leaders as follows:

> Reverence and unconditional obedience is due to the ministry of preaching when the preacher is ministering the Word of God. . . . Accordingly, when a preacher is ministering God's Word in his congregation, whether he be teaching or admonishing, reproving or comforting, publicly or privately, the congregation hears from his mouth Jesus Christ himself and owes him uncondi-

tional obedience as to a person by whom God wants to make known His will to them and guide them to eternal life. The more faithfully the preacher discharges his office, the greater must be the reverence of which the congregation deems him worthy.[42]

Walther adds, however, that the preacher may not dominate the church nor insist on obedience to himself in matters not commanded or forbidden by God's Word.[43]

All three aspects of obedience to evangelical authority—faith in the Gospel, holiness of life, respect for Gospel messengers—are elevating and beneficial to the obedient person. Edification rather than denigration is the result of such obedience. In fact, this obedience is a gift and work of God in the Christian, rather than a demand which He exacts. It is liberation from the condemnation and tyranny of sin, rather than bondage and repression to a hostile will. It is the rescue and restoration of the self, rather than its destruction. Although it is both a privilege and a duty, the accent is on privilege. The prospect of obeying evangelical authority should produce a response of joyful expectation rather than resentment or depression. The entire thrust of the discussion of this type of obedience in both Scripture and the Confessions is extremely positive.

NOTES TO CHAPTER II

[1] F.C., S.D. V, 20-21 (Tappert, pp. 561-562).
[2] L.C., 35-38 (Tappert, p. 415).
[3] F.C., S.D. V, 20-21 (Tappert, pp. 561-562).
[4] Ap. IV, 43-47 (Tappert, p. 113).
[5] Ap. XII, 76 (Tappert, p. 193). See also Luther's discussion of the Second Article L.C., 25-33 (Tappert, pp. 413-415).
[6] F.C., S.D. V (Tappert, pp. 538-563). On this subject see also C.F.W. Walther, *God's No and God's Yes: The Proper Distinction between Law and Gospel*, translated by W.H.T. Dau and condensed by Walter C. Pieper (Saint Louis: Concordia Publishing House, c. 1973).
[7] Edmund Schlink, *Theology of the Lutheran Confessions*, translated by Paul F. Koehneke and Herbert J.A. Bouman (Philadelphia: Fortress Press, c. 1961), Ch. III.
[8] Lk. 24:44-49. Analysis of the apostolic preaching in Acts reveals the extent to which the apostles and their associates preached Christ from the Old Testament: Acts 2:14-39, 3:17-26, 7:1-53, 8:26-35, 13:16-41. See also C.H. Dodd, *The Apostolic Preaching and Its Development* (New York: Harper and Brothers Publishers, c. 1936).

[9] Schlink, *op. cit.*, pp. 1-10.

[10] For example, the Upper Room discourses, Jn. 13-16.

[11] E.g., Rom. 6-8 and 12-14; most of 1 and 2 Cor., Gal. 5 and 6, Eph. 4-6, and most of the Pastoral Epistles (1 and 2 Tim. and Tit.).

[12] Much of the Johanine epistles and even Revelation.

[13] Rom. 12 is a good example: "I appeal to you therefore, brethren, *by the mercies of God* (emphasis added), to present your bodies as a living sacrifice. . ." The italicized phrase is a summary reference to the profound exposition of the Gospel given in the previous chapters. Chapters 12-15 then explain how the forgiven and transformed person is to act in a wide variety of morally significant situations. Phil. 2:1-13; 1 Jn. 4:7-12; 1 Pet. 2:11-3:18 are also good examples of Gospel imperatives, that is, moral instruction intimately related to Gospel affirmations.

[14] On this subject I know of no work in English more profound and helpful than Adolph Koeberle, *The Quest for Holiness*, translated by John C. Mattes (Minneapolis: Augsburg Publishing Company, c. 1936). Also see Schlink, *op. cit.*, Ch. 4.

[15] *Ibid.*, pp. 8-9.

[16] The most detailed discussion of this in the New Testament is found in the Pastoral Epistles (1 and 2 Tim. and Tit.). However, see also the charge of Paul to the Ephesian elders (Acts 20:28-35). Peter's charge to elders (1 Pet. 5:1-5), and the description of the Apostolic Council at work (Acts 15). Ch. III and IV of this book on "Confessional Authority" and "Disciplinary Authority" will consider the negative aspects of the ministry — polemics and excommunication.

[17] C.F.W. Walther, *Die Stimme unserer Kirche in der Frage von Kirche und Amt*, translated in *Walther and the Church*, by Wm. Dallmann, W.H.T. Dau, and Th. Engelder, ed. (Saint Louis: Concordia Publishing House, c. 1938), pp. 71-72.

[18] A.C. XXVIII, 1-21 (Tappert, pp. 81-84).

[19] A.C. V (Tappert, p. 31).

[20] S.A. III, iv (Tappert, p. 310), Tr., 24 (Tappert, p. 324).

[21] A.C. V (Tappert, p. 31), Tr., 60-69 (Tappert, pp. 330-331).

[22] Tr., 23-31 (Tappert, pp. 324-325).

[23] Ap. XIII, 7-13 (Tappert, pp. 212-213).

[24] Schlink, *op. cit.*, pp. 241-247.

[25] For example, 1 Pet. 1:13-2:10 and virtually the entire Epistle to the Ephesians.

[26] Tr., 22-31, 60-71 (Tappert, pp. 323-325, 330-332).

[27] The Corinthian correspondence best illustrates his deferential manner toward even a very difficult and recalcitrant congregation. Philemon illustrates his tactful way of eliciting a response to the Gospel from an individual.

[28] A.C. XXVIII, 21-22 (Tappert, p. 84).

[29] *Ibid.*, 19-20 (Tappert, pp. 83-84).

[30] One of the most offensive examples of this was the severe penalties imposed against priests who married contrary to church regulations, A.C. XXIII, 18-23 (Tappert, pp. 54-55).

[31] Ap. XXVIII, 6 (Tappert, p. 282).

[32] A.C. XXVIII, 34-52 (Tappert, pp. 86-89).

[33] *Ibid.*, 21 (Tappert, p. 84).

[34] "Synodalrede," *Missouri Synod Proceedings, 1848*, pp. 30-38 (2nd ed.), trans., Paul F. Koehneke, "Dr. Walther's First Presidential Address," *Concordia Historical Institute Quarterly*, XXXIII (April 1960), 12-20.

[35] Ap. IV, 227-228 (Tappert, pp. 138-139).

[36] F.C., S.D. III, 8-16 (Tappert, pp. 540-541).

[37] Ap. IV, 126-144 (Tappert, pp. 124-127).

[38] F.C., Ep. IV, 5-11 (Tappert, pp. 476-477).

[39] Schlink, *op. cit.*, pp. 105-116.

[40] A.C. XXVIII, 22 (Tappert, p. 84).

[41] L.C., 158-165 (Tappert, p. 387).

[42] *Walther and the Church*, p. 80.

[43] *Ibid.*, pp. 81-83.

P
AUTHORITY
confessional

Chapter III

Confessional Authority

Christians have the privilege and responsibility to communicate the Gospel. In Chapter II this was designated and described as "evangelical authority," because it is essentially the authority to evangelize. In this chapter we focus on a second aspect of authority in the church. It is confessional authority: the privilege and responsibility to proclaim the Gospel *over against current heresy.*

Personal Affirmation in the Face of Hostility and Error

The word "confession" in common usage most often refers to admission of sin or guilt. Although that is not entirely excluded in the concept of confessional authority, neither is it the major thrust. In this case, we are referring to confession as a declaration or acknowledgment of faith, that is to say, of the object of Christian faith, which is the Gospel of Jesus Christ. Confessional authority, like evangelical authority, is the right and the duty to bear witness to the Gospel. However, there is also a distinction between them. If the term is used with precision, "confession" emphasizes the *personal commitment of the witness* to that which is proclaimed. In the case of Christian confession the spokesperson not only says, "Jesus gave Himself for you," he also adds in some way, "and I believe this myself and am counting on Jesus for my salvation." Witness becomes confession when the witness reveals that this is his/her personal conviction. Another characteristic element of confession is that it is an affirmation made over against error or hostility. It is witness to Christ under these kinds of pressure. Confession is saying, "The Gospel in which I believe is this, *not* that." False and distorted versions of the Gospel are noted and rejected. The contrast between the authentic Gospel and its counterfeits is clearly drawn. Witness also becomes confession when it is given in the face of opposition – to those who reject or persecute the Gospel.[1]

Examination of the New Testament passages which employ the words "to confess" (ὁμολογεῖν) and "confession" (ὁμολογία) discloses this latter meaning. After describing in frightening detail the persecution that they could expect when they spoke and acted as His representatives, Jesus said to His apostles, "So everyone who acknowledges (confesses) me before men, I also will acknowledge (confess) before my Father who is in heaven; but whoever denies me before men, I also will deny before my Father who is in Heaven (Matt. 10:32-33). To confess Christ, then, is not only to preach about Him but to identify oneself with Him to claim and own Him regardless of the consequences.

That confession is also affirmation over against false views can be illustrated by the response of John the Baptist to those who were inclined to identify him as the Christ: "He confessed, he did not deny but confessed, "I am not the Christ," (Jn.1:20). He specifically rejected their false interpretation of the Gospel—that he, John, was the Messiah, and directed them instead to Jesus, the true Savior (Jn. 1:19-34). In his defense before Felix, Paul said, "I admit (confess) to you, that according to the Way which they call a sect, I worship the God of our fathers. . ." (Acts 25:14). Here, too, confession involves emphasis on personal commitment as well as affirmation in the face of error and hostility.

Elsewhere Paul referred to the good confession which Timothy made and compared it with the confession of Jesus before Pontius Pilate (1 Tim. 6:12-13). This comparison implies the key elements of confession to which we have called attention. As Jesus had clearly identified Himself to Pilate (Jn. 18:36-38) Timothy had identified himself as one of Jesus' own. As Jesus' confession was made over against the false views of Pilate and His enemies and in the face of danger, Timothy, too, stood up for Jesus to those who distorted and opposed Him. The apostle urged Timothy to continue in this confession. The author to the Hebrews after exhorting his readers to recognize and resist false teaching (13:9) and to be willing to bear abuse for Jesus (13:13) adds, "Through him then let us continually offer up a sacrifice of praise to God, that is, the fruit of lips that acknowledge (confess) His name" (13:15).

One aspect of confession that is particularly important for the development of the thought of this chapter is the polemical. The positive work of evangelizing must be combined with the negative work of polemicizing. That is to say, as we communicate the Gospel truth we must also expose and condemn every error that contradicts, twists, obscures, or undercuts that truth. Jesus' own preaching included a sharp polemic, especially against the Scribes and the Pharisees (e.g. Matt. 23). Paul's preaching was severly critical especially of the Judaizers (e.g. Gal. and Phil. 3:2-11). John combined his beautiful message of God's love with an attack against those who denied the incarnation (1 Jn. 2:18-25, 4:1-3, 5:6-12).

Other church leaders, furthermore, were alerted to the threat of false teachers and teaching (Acts 20:29-30; 1 Tim. 4:1-5, 6:3-6; 2 Tim. 3). While unwholesome preoccupation with these errors was forbidden, and avoidance of the errorists were counseled (1 Tim. 1:4, 4:7; 2 Tim. 2:14-18; Rom. 16:17) Christians were to speak the truth in love over against them (Eph. 4:14-15), to charge errorists to cease and desist (1 Tim. 1:3), guard the truth that had been entrusted to them (2 Tim. 1:14), refute and correct error with Scripture (2 Tim. 3:16; Tit. 1:9), and thus to "contend for the faith which was once for all delivered to the saints" (Jude 3).

There is much more to confession than polemics. Confession is, above all, the affirmation of the Gospel and identification with Jesus Christ. The scriptural evidence cited, however, indicates that polemics (refutation) is also a valid and important part of the confessional right and duty. We are authorized and expected by God to affirm the Gospel over against current heresy. That is confessional authority as discussed in this presentation.

The Lutheran Confessional Writings do not contain an explicit doctrine about the nature of a confession. A definition may be inferred, though, from a variety of related comments and by the doctrinal contents of the Confessions. The Confessions claim to be the church's normative exposition of the whole and heart of Scripture, that is the Gospel, as defined over against current heresy. They are a response to Scripture which indicates how Christians, the churches, understand and express the meaning of Scripture. That meaning is centered in and integrated by the good news of Jesus, in conjunction with the diagnostic and condemning message of the law. A confession is the product of a particular age and situation. It states how the church at a given time perceived and proclaimed the Scriptural Gospel in the face of false and dangerous errors which were being proposed.

The appearance of heresies is what stimulates and necessitates the production of confessional documents. However, the heresies do not contribute to the substance of the Confessions, only to their form. And, Confessions remain valid even after the heresy under attack has disappeared. Heresy is not simply the product of human fallibility and finitude. It is the work of the devil by which he attempts to deceive and dominate human beings. Hence, in a very real sense, confession is doing battle against the devil. The Confessions are not an authority over Scripture or even equal to Scripture. They are a witness to Scripture, explanations of Scripture, as well as models to aid others in their understanding and teaching of Scripture.[2]

Necessity of Confessions

The necessity of confessions, i.e., the duty of affirming the Scriptural Gospel over against error, is strongly asserted. The last of the Lutheran Confessions, The Formula of Concord, explains why. Just as there were controversies in the apostolic church because of the intrusion of error, so in the churches of the Augsburg Confession some theologians had deviated from the truth either deliberately or ignorantly. Controversies and divisions had resulted. The disagreements were not mere misunderstandings with the parties talking past each other, nor contentions about very minor points. Rather, they centered in doctrines of such importance and involved errors of such magnitude that the deviant opinions could not be tolerated in the church of God, much less excused or defended. Among the errors under consideration were the views that good works are necessary to salvation, that Christ's body and blood are not present in the sacrament, and that the law of God is not a guide for the Christian life.

The Formula of Concord, prepared after prolonged discussion and repeated revision, demonstrated from Scripture and earlier Lutheran Confessions which views in the controversies were correct, "so that well meaning Christians who are really concerned about the truth may know how to guard and protect themselves against the errors and corruption that have invaded our midst."[3] When serious doctrinal errors appear in the church, people need help in evaluating them so as not to be led astray. It is the duty of spiritual leaders to provide such assistance. Once peace and unity have been restored, the message of the church, that is the Scriptural Gospel, must be kept sound and whole by continuous confession against everything which contradicts it.

> In order to preserve the pure doctrine and to maintain a thorough, lasting, and God-pleasing concord within the church, it is essential not only to present the

> true and wholesome doctrine correctly, but also to accuse the adversaries who teach otherwise (1 Tim. 3:9; Tit. 1:9; 2 Tim. 2:24, 3:16). "Faithful shepherds," as Luther states, "must both pasture or feed the lambs and guard against wolves so that they will flee from strange voices and separate the precious from the vile"(Jn. 10:12-16,27; Jer.15:19).[4]

Creeds and Confessions are the product of the church's exercise of confessional authority. At various points in history, the church has confronted those who, claiming to base their views on Scripture, have, in fact, radically departed from the truth of the Gospel. In response to them, the church has turned to Scripture, absorbed its meaning, and then articulated that meaning in such a way as to indicate how it differs from the novel and unsatisfactory views of the heretics. The Lutheran Confessions were efforts in the Sixteenth Century comparable to the three general creeds of the early church. They express the Lutheran perception of Scriptural truth over against the inadequate and erroneous views held at that time by Roman Catholics, Reformed, Anabaptists, and a variety of cults and sects as well as those in the Lutheran fold who had departed from the truth.[5]

Historic Confessions and the Contemporary Church

The contemporary church in its various manifestations—congregations, synods, etc.—may select and adopt earlier creeds and confessions. By their very nature creedal and confessional documents invite this. They propose to be, not merely personal and sectarian expressions of temporary significance, but rather the teaching of the faith of the whole church, past and present, which is normative for posterity as well as for contemporaries.

> Whoever wishes to be saved must, above all else, hold the true Christian faith. Whoever does not keep it whole and undefiled will without doubt perish for eternity. . . This is the true Christian faith. Unless a man believe this firmly and faithfully, he cannot be saved.[6]

> We consider this Confession (Augsburg) a genuinely Christian symbol *which all true Christians ought to accept next to the Word of God*, just as in ancient times Christian symbols and confessions were formulated in the church of God when great controversies broke out, and orthodox teachers and hearers pledged themselves to these symbols with heart and mouth.[7] (emphasis added)

> This agreement we have set forth as a certain and public testimony, not only to our contemporaries but also to our posterity, of that which our churches

believe and accept with one accord as the correct and abiding answer in the controverted issues... [8]

The church in every age is challenged to examine its confessional heritage, to test out these lofty claims. By a penetrating study of Scripture it is to determine whether or not the Gospel as presented in these documents is, in fact, the Scriptural Gospel and the rejected views are, in fact, serious and pernicious errors. Not a blind and mindless acceptance of tradition, but a responsible evaluation and appropriation of the Christian heritage on the basis of scriptural study is what the Confessions try to stimulate.

When confessional subscription is the result of such a process, it is valid and meaningful. In our study and exposition of Scripture and dealing with heresy, we do not try to start from scratch or go it alone. We try to benefit from the study and experience of those who have gone before, our spiritual ancestors. We hear them out carefully and respectfully. We compare their teaching with what Scripture itself says. Then, as individual Christians or collectively in our church organizations we may be moved by the Holy Spirit to say: "We, too, are people of this view and commitment. This is the way we perceive and express the Scriptural message. We, too, feel compelled to reject and condemn what is here refuted. We gladly and willingly pledge ourselves to teach and preach according to this model."

Continuing Confrontation with Heresy

Distortion and contradiction of the Scriptural Gospel did not end in the Sixteenth Century with the publication of the *Book of Concord*. Many of the views rejected in the Confessions have persisted in one form or another until the present. Moreover, new heresies have appeared, in some cases radically different from anything confronted by the Confessors, and these, too, must be answered. Confessional authority belongs to Twentieth Century Christians no less than to Sixteenth or Fourth Century Christians. We, too, have the right and the duty to speak out for God's Incarnate and Written Word and against everything which denies or corrupts it. As we do this the Confessions remain a vital and valuable resource, especially when the errors with which we are contending are related or similar to those to which the Confessors replied.

Even when we are dealing with novel heresies, totally outside the experience of the Confessors, they can assist us by the model of doing confessional theology which they provide. From them we can learn that all theological expression should be based on Scripture and centered in Christ. When evaluating and replying to questionable views, if we conform to the model of the Confessors, we will be guided by the questions: are these views consistent and compatible with Scripture? Do they express, support, or magnify the Gospel, or do they detract from it? Not one of these questions or the other, but both must be considered, if the model of the Confessions is to be followed. Since error continues in every age, confession must be made in every age, and the historic Confessions assist us in doing this.

It is unrealistic and unconfessional to imagine that the historic creeds and Confessions must be the last efforts of this kind undertaken by Christians. If the devil continually stirs up error in ever new forms, Christians must be prepared to reaffirm the Gospel over against these errors in ever new forms. To whatever extent they are relevant, the Confessions must be used, just as all the Confessions draw upon the Ancient Creeds and the later Confessions cite the earlier Confessions. However, we must also be willing to carry the discussion beyond that of the Confessions. If the necessity arises, we must be willing to make new Confessions or to augment the existing ones.

This view is itself controversial. "No new Confessions!" has become something of a battle cry. Certainly, great caution and restraint are appropriate in this area. Serious problems of procedure make the formulation of new confessions difficult. At this point we merely wish to affirm the principle that Christians of every age possess confessional authority and that this also includes the right and the duty to draw up new confessional statements, or, at least, binding interpretations of the historic Confessions. Schlink says:

> No Confession of the church may be regarded as definitive in the sense of precluding the possibility of further Confessions. All the Confessions had their origin in confrontation with errors — this fact is inherent in the very concept of a Confession, as the Confessions themselves and particularly the programmatic introduction to the Formula of Concord expressly declare — and to admit this is to acknowledge that the Book of Concord cannot be regarded as the final and conclusive Confession. At the very least the church, confronted with new heresies, will have to furnish up-to-date and binding interpretations of her official Confessions. But also beyond this we must soberly reckon with

> the possibility, perhaps even the necessity, of meeting the invasion of new errors with the formulation and validation of new Confessions.[9]

Some Analysis and Opinions About the Current Scene

Recent confessional attempts of the Lutheran Church-Missouri Synod, for example, could be evaluated in the light of this principle. Do Missouri Synod Christians, for instance, have the authority to draw up new confessional statements or to make binding interpretations of their existing Confessions? At this point we are not asking for a judgment on the quality or adequacy of the documents which have been produced and endorsed. Rather we are asking about the right of this or any group of Christians to attempt anything of the sort. On the basis of the evidence presented above it would seem that, convinced as they are of the seriousness of the doctrinal deviations with which they are confronted, they have not only the right but also the duty to act confessionally. No to do so would be to permit error to go unchallenged and the truth of the Gospel to be obscured.

Furthermore, the confessional actions taken by the Synod, if viewed dispassionately, appear to make rather modest claims and demands. These actions center around the adoption of *A Statement of Scriptural and Confessional Principles* at the New Orleans Convention, July 6-13, 1973. How do those who formulated and adopted the pertinent resolution interpret their intentions and actions? Resolution 3-01 states that *A Statement* is consistent both with Scripture and Confessions and expresses the Synod's position on current doctrinal issues. The resolution explains that since *A Statement* was published and available for study well in advance of that convention it is to be regarded as a more formal and comprehensive expression of belief than a doctrinal resolution simply formulated and adopted at a convention.[10] Clarification of this and similar resolutions was given at the Anaheim Convention, July 4-11, 1975. Resolution 3-04 states:

> In order to give witness to its faith in the face of contemporary issues and in order to settle controversies within its own midst, the Synod has the right to adopt doctrinal resolutions and to ask its members to uphold them. In doing so the Synod cannot and does not establish new doctrines but merely gives joyful assent to what in its conviction is taught in the sacred Scriptures. Indeed, *insofar* as such resolutions are in accord with the Scriptures they are

binding on those who accept Article II of Synod's Constitution.[11] (emphasis added)

The very next Anaheim resolution (3-05) explains that the New Orleans Resolution 3-01 did not create a new Confession, but simply defines the corporate position of the Synod and sets forth the public teaching of the Synod. It also assures that the Synod can not make *A Statement* binding in the same sense in which Scripture and the Confessions are binding. Members of Synod are, however, to honor and uphold the doctrinal content of this document, which means that they are to examine, study and teach and act in accordance with it until it "shall have been shown to be contrary to God's Word."[12] No claim of infallibility is made. The document is, according to this same resolution, subject to correction and improvement. It is subordinate to Scripture and the Confessions, and merely seeks to express the consensus of the Synod on how these authorities are to be interpreted on controverted points. In short, *A Statement* appears to be what Schlink calls an up-to-date and binding interpretation of the Synod's official Confessions.

Is this a valid and necessary exercise of confessional authority? The answer will depend on one's assessment of the views and doctrines against which *A Statement* speaks. On the one hand, those who are convinced that these matters are open questions, matters of historical or exegetical opinion, which in no way call the Gospel or the authority of Scripture into question, view the adoption of this document as an unwarranted infringement upon their Christian liberty. They see it as a dangerous move to suppress the scholarly study of the Bible, and an un-Lutheran elevation of Scripture over the Gospel. On the other hand, its proponents view the positions opposed and rejected in *A Statement* as an assault against the authority of the Bible and, consequently, against the Gospel itself, since the Bible is God's own inspired record of the Gospel events. They view the adoption of *A Statement* as the least that the Synod could do in the responsible exercise of its confessional authority.

Evangelical Authority and Organizational Authority in Conjunction

When Christians exercise confessional authority, when they act collectively to affirm the Gospel over against error, they are operating also with several other forms of authority considered in this study. To the extent that they are proclaiming the Gospel in their Confession, they are exercising evangelical authority (Chapter II). To the extent that they are working through their organizational structure and making corporate decisions and embodying these in various kinds of regulations, they are exercising organizational authority (Chapter V). The exercise of organizational authority includes the use of human reason and sanctified common sense. Like everything else human, corporate attitudes and actions are also tainted by sin. These human factors in organizational authority are what make us susceptible to error and injustice even when we are striving to speak God's truth in love. These human factors impose clear limits on what we may attempt to do in the exercise of confessional authority. We may not create doctrines or articles of faith. That is God's sole prerogative. Our sinfulness, fallibility, and finitude make us incapable of doing the work of revelation.

However, we can and must confess that truth which God has revealed to us in Christ and Scripture. This puts the confessional decisions and expressions of Christians in a unique category. Because they are a communication of God's revelation they are more than just human opinion and judgments. Because they involve human interpretation and analysis, however, they are less than divine revelation. They are a human response to God's revelation in reaction to something which appears to deny or pervert it.[13] *Insofar* as they are in accord with Scripture they are binding. Accordance with Scripture, though, is not something which may be assumed. Confessional documents must be evaluated and tested against Scripture and its Gospel norm. They must be scrutinized for the intrusion of human opinion and error or false emphases, and accepted only after their soundness has been thoroughly established.[14] To subscribe to confessional documents is to express conviction that they have passed this test.

Confession and Consensus

The exercise of confessional authority in the form of a confessional statement implies a consensus. It is an action which a group of Christians take together. As they reflect upon and discuss the controversial issues, as they study Scripture as well as the creeds and confessions of their spiritual forebearers, Christians arrive at agreement about what is true and to be believed and taught in their midst, and about what is false and to be opposed. This agreement is not something that develops, first of all, in the councils of the church or among its leaders. It is a common conviction which grows out of teaching and preaching, out of study and discussion that take place in the schools and congregations of the church. Not only the ministers but also the laity are engaged in this process.

The consensus that emerges is regarded—not merely as human preference or opinion, but rather as a perception and conviction of what God Himself reveals and wills through His Word. To the extent that the persons involved in the process are using God's Word and responding to God's Word, the consensus is the work of the Holy Spirit. Sooner or later the larger assemblies of the church also become involved. Someone, it does not matter whether it is an individual or a committee, puts pen to paper in an attempt to articulate the consensus which has emerged or is emerging. In the appropriate forums the document is considered, and it is either accepted in its original or a revised form, or it is rejected. The basis on which it is accepted is that it is regarded as an accurate and definitive statement of God's truth over against these errors *as we have already come*—in the wording of the Lutheran Confessions—*to believe, teach, and confess it in our churches.* The Confession is not only what we think *ought* to be taught. It is what we are, in fact, saying and teaching right now. By the formulation and adoption of a confessional document Christians claim to exhibit a consensus previously attained at the grass roots by extensive study, reflection, and discussion.[15]

Confessional documents are of different types, and they possess different kinds of authority. Most authoritative are the three creeds produced by the early church (Apostles, Nicene, and Athanasian), because they represent the consensus of ancient and undivided Christendom. Next, for Lutherans, come the Lutheran Confessional Writings of the Sixteenth Century, appended to the ancient creeds in the *Book of Concord.* The Lutheran Confessions were drawn up during the formative years of Lutheranism and represent a very large concensus. The vast majority of Lutherans then and subsequently have subscribed them. Although distinctively Lutheran, they also claim to be consistent with and expressive of the faith and witness of the universal church down through the ages. They present themselves as the church's normative exposition of the entirety and heart of Scripture, namely, the Gospel, not only for their own time but also for posterity.

Documents of a confessional nature drawn up by Post-Reformation Lutherans have been regarded as subordinate to the Confessions as well as to Scripture. These more recent confessional expressions have been viewed as *interpretations and applications* of Scripture and the Confessions to issues and problems not covered explicitly in them. They represent a smaller consensus, that is, the consensus of a smaller segment of Lutheranism than did those of the Sixteenth Century. In many cases, those later documents are regarded as more tentative. They are subject to revision, correction, and improvement, in contrast to the classic Confessions which make some claim to finality and have been guarded against change down through the ages.[16]

A distinction may be made between the Confessions and a consensus. Although the Confessions represent a consensus, not every consensus in the church of a doctrinal nature is on a par with the Confessions. The Confessions contain what may be termed "articles of faith," that is to say, those affirmations of the Scriptural Gospel in its fulness, which are to be believed and taught without qualification or equivocation because they are based on very clear and complete biblical testimony.

From time to time groups of Christians consider and come to a consensus about matters not taught so clearly and completely in Scripture. This consensus may include moral judgments (e.g., regarding abortion), or historical and exegetical judgments (e.g., the historicity of Jonah), or theological-practical conclusions (e.g., views and regulations about fellowship with other Christians). Christians may formulate, adopt, and publish their collective conclusions and opinions on these matters and even agree that teaching and preaching in their midst will conform to this consensus. However, to the extent that this consensus lacks adequate and conclusive Scriptural support, it is not an article of faith. It is the considered opinion of the group about a question that is regarded very seriously. It may be binding in the sense that members, in the interest of harmony, are asked and expected to honor and uphold it. However, it lacks finality, and it is subject to change and improvement, if further study, reflection, and experience of the group so indicate.

Ecclesiastical doctrinal resolutions are expressions of consensus with confessional significance. They are an attempt to affirm the Scriptural Gospel over against current heresy. However, they do not possess full confessional status. Failure to distinguish between articles of faith and the current consensus has created considerable confusion in many Christian groups including the Lutheran Church-Missouri Synod.

Consensus, of course, is never complete. Because of the human factors in the confessional process, there will always be some who disagree profoundly with the conclusions of the majority. There will be others who are dissatisfied to some extent and in some ways with the articulation of the consensus in the confessional document. A vast consensus was expressed in the earliest Lutheran Confessions. At least, such a consensus was attained during the half-century after their issuance:

> The reason why we have embodied the writings listed above—the Augsburg Confessions, the Apology, the Smalcald Articles, and Luther's Large and Small Catechisms—in the cited summary of our Christian doctrine is that they *have always and everywhere been accepted* as the common and universally accepted belief of our churches, that the chief and most illustrious theologians of that time subscribed them, and that all Evangelical churches and schools received them.[17] (emphasis added)

Actually, there was some dissent from the very beginning. Already at Augsburg (1530), for instance, four major evangelical cities with Reformed leanings issued their Tetrapolitan Confession as an alternative to the Augsburg Confession, thus initiating a drift away from the Lutherans.[18] Also, Luther's Smalcald Articles (1537) were not endorsed officially at the meeting for which they are named, but only signed privately by many of the clergymen present. This was engineered by Melanchthon who thereby hoped to prevent further alienation of these cities. He feared that Luther's forthright affirmation of Christ's sacramental presence in these articles would offend people with Reformed sympathies. Only in later years did the Smalcald Articles gain general confessional status.[19]

The consensus represented by the Formula of Concord, the document which helped to resolve the controversies raging among the Lutherans themselves, was even smaller. By 1580, a half-century after Augsburg, when the Formula was published in its final form in the *Book of Concord*, 8,188 theologians, ministers, and teachers[20] and a decided majority of Lutheran cities and states had subscribed it. In all, about two-thirds of the Lutherans in Germany identified with this confession. Not all who withheld their subscription disagreed doctrinally with the Formula. Some did so out of animosity toward the authors of the Formula or their princes.[21] Still today a significant number of Lutherans decline subscription, in many cases because they feel that the discussion of Christology in Articles VII and VIII goes beyond or is inconsistent with what is said in the earlier Lutheran Confessions.[22] In any case, complete consensus was not attained even with regard to the historic Lutheran Confessions.

More Opinions About the Present

Nor can a complete consensus realistically be expected in the confessional process today. For example, that there is disagreement with and dissent from the Missouri Synod's recent confessional actions and statement is to be expected. The important questions appear to be: what is the basis of the dissatisfaction and dissent? Is it personal animosity toward the author(s) or the documents? Is it concern about the constitutionality of the resolution for adoption? Is it fear that the resolutions and documents will be misused? Is it substantive deviation from the contents of the documents? Is it conviction on the part of the dissenters that this statement is contrary to the Scriptures and the Gospel: that it fails to deal adequately with the problems it proposes to address? Is it the result of pressing for acceptance of *A Statement* before there was sufficient time and opportunity to consider and discuss and revise it? Was it all of the above? In this case, as in the interpretation of most human events, multiple causation seems most plausible. The reasons for dissent are doubtless numerous, complex, and subtle, and, therefore, difficult to pin down with precision.

In order to respond to dissent and dissenters in the most appropriate and effective manner, one must first of all try to understand them as well as he possibly can. The analysis should not only be rigorous; it should also be sensitive, loving, fair, and open. Dissenters are, after all, sometimes correct, and a large consensus can be wrong. The first Christians were dissenters from traditional Judaism. The first Lutherans were dissenters from Medieval Roman Catholicism. Those who are now the controlling majority in the Missouri Synod were at one time an embattled and dissenting minority.

As brothers and sisters in Christ, dissenters deserve a hearing. Their positions, complaints, and criticism deserve serious consideration. Whatever is valid in their position should be recognized and accepted. Their just complaints should be satisfied. Every effort should be made to deal with the personal conflicts which inevitably add bitterness and vehemence to the controversy. Discussion and reflection so vital to the attainment and maintenance of unity should not be cut short by panic or impatience. Discussion of the issues should be carried out in a non-threatening context, so that participants can afford to say what they really think and believe. None of this should involve the surrender or sacrifice of truth. Rather, it should be a process of seeking and speaking the truth in love.

For their part, dissenters need in a humble and open manner to consider the confessional expression of the majority. They need to try to understand as accurately as possible what the majority are saying, why they are saying it, and what they mean by it. They need to be generous and trusting, putting the best construction on everything. Dissenters need to avoid rebellious words and deeds, to be as willing to recognize faults and errors in themselves as in the other party. In none of this should they violate their consciences or compromise their vision of the truth. Instead, they should relate lovingly with those whose positions and actions they are challenging.[23]

Purpose of Confessional Expression

Christians have a dual purpose in speaking or writing confessionally. First of all, they wish to *exhibit a unity* of doctrine, a common perception and conviction of the Scriptural Gospel. To one another and to other Christians and to the world, they wish to project a sharply focused picture of God's love in Christ, which they share over against the conflicting and inadequate pictures which some others are projecting. In this they are, in fact, demonstrating the one-ness which the Holy Spirit has accomplished among them, "the unity of the Spirit" (Eph. 4:3). Grateful for His work of revelation and clarification, eager to glorify Him and to communicate to others their consensus in the Gospel which He has created, they articulate it in carefully chosen words, usually written.

However, there is also another purpose and that is to *foster unity of doctrine*. By the clear and united statement of the truth Christians try to dissuade those who are enmeshed in or inclined toward error. They attempt to refute the errorists, so that others will not be taken in by them and their teaching. Left unanswered, error may well spread and worsen. Confessors try to draw the lines between truth and error boldly and clearly. The Scriptural Gospel itself, of course, needs no protection. It is God's own weapon against error and sin of every kind. We do not protect the Gospel; it protects us and others. Confession does not protect the Gospel. Rather, confession is an affirmation of the Gospel over against current heresy in order to promote unity and to protect people from counterfeit gospels. The unity of the church is much more than merely doctrinal and confessional unity. It is the personal and organic unity of the Body of Christ, the bond that exists among all believers because of their common faith in Jesus Christ. This is more than confessional unity, but not less. Confessional unity expresses, clarifies, and deepens the unity of the Body of Christ: "The unity of the church does not exist without the unity of creed."[24]

Consensus must be cultivated. It can not be decreed. Whenever consensus is attained, it may be announced and celebrated. Others may be invited to share the consensus. There is no way, however, to legislate a consensus. Shared convictions are not created by organizational fiat or regulation. Christian minds and consciences are drawn together by the Holy Spirit through Baptism, the Word, and the Eucharist (Acts 2:37-47, 4:32). To a limited degree, however, consensus may be protected by organizational decisions and actions of Christians. They may agree to control the amount of false or questionable doctrine which is permitted in their midst. Out of regard for the truth of the Gospel, the spiritual well-being of Christians, and also the unity of the church, they may designate some views as intolerable in the church of God.[25]

Such controls can not be completely effective. If they wish, people can always hear and read such condemned views outside the structures of the church. Furthermore, some exposure to such views may be necessary for people, if only to warn them. However, in order to protect the consensus Christians may and should limit the input of dissenting and deviant doctrine (Rom. 16:17; 1 Tim.

1:3, 6:3-6, 20-21). There is a point at which dissenting views may and should be considered and discussed. This was described above. However, when a group of Christians comes to the conviction that a certain view is dangerously false, seriously at odds with the Scripture and the Gospel, then that view must be repressed in the interest of truth and unity. If error is given equal opportunity with truth, it may mislead the weak; the consensus may be shattered and chaos may prevail.

Obedience to Confessional Authority

Obedience, we have said repeatedly, is appropriate response to authority. The form of obedience is determined largely by the nature of the authority which it confronts. Because confessional authority is a unique kind of authority, obedience to it takes a unique form.

Confessional authority is the privilege and responsibility to affirm the Gospel over against current heresy. This involves a process: (1) confrontation with suspect views, (2) analysis of them on the basis of Scripture and already established Confessions, (3) decision regarding their acceptability or non-acceptability, (4) articulation of the correct Scriptural teaching, and, (5) rejection of that which is judged false. This process is to be carried out on the individual and congregational levels as well as in the larger assemblies of the church. It is to involve the laity as well as the clergy and the theologians. It is to result ultimately in a consensus, and, in most cases, a statement or document.

This formal confession may merely be commended to the members for their consideration and guidance. It may be made binding in the sense that they are required to honor and uphold it. It may even be given full confessional status, if the Scriptural basis is sufficiently clear and complete and the consensus large enough. How much is "enough" has never been specified and, perhaps, never can be. It is a determination which Christians must make in the freedom of faith in a concrete situation.

If this is confessional authority, what form does obedience take with reference to it? It can *not* take the form of implicit trust or mindless acceptance of the decisions of others. It can not be a matter of simply letting a church body or its leaders or assemblies tell me what to believe and to reject. It can not be merely a matter of following and supporting the opinions of one's pastor.

The tendency, even the temptation, to view obedience to the confessional authority of the church in those ways is strong. The issues are complex. Unbiased information is difficult to obtain. Many lack time as well as an adequate level of theological training to think and act with either confidence or independence. People grow weary of the controversies; they long to concentrate on something more positive. If, however, confessional authority is a duty as well as a right, and if it belongs to all Christians and not only to the ecclesiastical elite, then obedience can not take such passive forms.

Obedience to confessional authority is, first of all, involvement in the confessional process at whatever level ability, training, time, and opportunity allow. After all, confessional expressions deal not only with what is taught in the colleges and seminaries of the church, but also with what is communicated in the pulpits and schools of the church. Those with lesser theological training should no more be intimidated into a passive role in the confessional process than they should arrogantly or presumptuously reject the contributions of the theologians. They should participate conscientiously in the process. They should analyse and judge suspect views on the basis of their best knowledge of the Bible and the Confessions, and they should also carefully evaluate whatever is proposed as an answer to these views.

On the basis of such participation, individuals, congregations, and even groups of congregations must *either accept or reject the consensus that results from this process.* Obedience to confessional authority is ultimately obedience to the Scriptural Gospel in its fullness. If after serious and prayerful consideration, participants are convinced that a confessional expression is significantly deviant from the Scripture and its Gospel norm, then obedience will consist in rejecting that document or resolution, regardless of the consequences, and making a different Confession. If, on the other hand, the persons involved are satisfied that the expression is both valid and necessary, obedience for them consists in identifying with it, and teaching and witnessing in accordance with it.

only a ministry of the law. It is a
s law in conjunction with and in the
to make people aware of their sins
open to and interested in the forgiv-
g power of the Gospel. In exercising
urch is like a physician who must jar
direct and frightening diagnosis, so
he radical treatment which is needed.

Keys

ipture which corresponds precisely to
inary authority. The various stages of
well as the manner in which they are re-
New Testament, as will be shown. The
mpts to gather these elements into a single
s do something similar to this. They speak
tion" which is defined as "the authority to
ho are guilty of public offenses or to absolve
rted and ask for absolution."[1] These public
doctrinal or moral. Those who exercise this
rine and condemn doctrine that is contrary
xclude from the Christian community those
t is manifest."[2] That the false teacher is to be
is teaching is also affirmed: "We should for-
because they no longer function in the place
ichrists."[3]

risdiction, the confessors' equivalent of disci-
is part of a larger authority called "the Office of
explains that the keys are a function and power
h to bind and loose sins.[4] "To bind" means not
l "to loose sins" means to forgive.[5] The keys are
mforting promise of forgiveness, the absolution,
n the Confessions are described only in terms of
owever, they also include the expression of God's
nt. They involve the retention as well as the remis-
is this negative dimension of the Office of the Keys
fessions call "the power of jurisdiction." The posi-
n, the proclamation of the Gospel, which we have

NOTES TO CHAPTER III

[1] I do not mean to suggest that this distinction between confession (ὁμολογία) and witness (μαρτυρία) and their corresponding verb forms is observed consistently in the New Testament. Witnessing is and must be done in the face of danger — one who suffers or dies for his testimony is a martyr. Furthermore, witness can also be given against someone or something false or evil. The concept of witness may also include reference to the personal experience and conviction of the spokesperson. The distinction is rather a matter of emphasis. Confession *tends* to be a more general form of Gospel declaration.

[2] Edmund Schlink, *Theology of the Lutheran Confessions*, trans. by Paul F. Koehneke and Herbert J.A. Bouman, (Philadelphia: Fortress Press, c. 1961) Introduction and Ch. 1.

[3] F.C., S.D., Intro., 6-10 (Tappert, pp. 502-503).

[4] *Ibid.*, Antitheses to the Controverted Articles, 14 (Tappert, p. 506).

[5] *Ibid.*, Sum. Form. (Tappert, pp. 503-506).

[6] Anthanasian Creed 1, 2, and 40 (Tappert, pp. 19 and 21).

[7] F.C., S.D., Sum. Form., 4 (Tappert, p. 502).

[8] Ibid., 16 (Tappert, p. 507).

[9] Schlink, *op. cit.,* p. 31. Not only the quotation but the discussion of this entire section follows Schlink, pp. 31-32.

[10] *Convention Proceedings*, pp. 127-128.

[11] *Convention Proceedings*, p. 95.

[12] *Ibid.*, and pp. 96-97.

[13] Tr., 56 (Tappert, pp. 329-330).

[14] F.C., Ep., Comp. Sum., 1-2 (Tappert, pp. 464-465).

[15] A.C. Pref., 8 (Tappert, p. 25); S.A. Signatories (Tappert, pp. 316-318); Preface to the Book of Concord (Tappert, pp. 1-14).

[16] Schlink, *op. cit.*, Intro.

[17] F.C., S.D. Sum. Form., 11 (Tappert, p. 506).

[18] Williston Walker, *A History of the Christian Church* (New York: Charles Scribner's Sons, c. 1970), p. 334.

[19] Willard Dow Allbeck, *Studies in the Lutheran Confessions* (Philadelphia: Fortress Press, c. 1968), pp. 193-194.

[20] F.C., Intro. (Tappert, p. 464).

[21] Allbeck, *op. cit.*, pp. 258-259.

[22] Schlink, *op. cit.*, pp. xxvi and 192.

[23] In order to understand why it is necessary to spell out with some specificity what it means to act and speak in love in a situation of confessional disagreement, the reader need only consider the frequency and seriousness with which parties on both sides violate this.

[24] Schlink, *op. cit.*, p. 206; 1 Cor. 1:10-13; F.C., S.D. Sum. Form., 13-14 (Tappert, p. 506).

[25] F.C., S.D., Intro., 6-10 (Tappert, pp. 502-503).

e
er
pe
abov
those
cern,
and ob
those w
ciplinary

Like
sidered, d
the Gospel.
to those who
lost it. The m
ity is to be lov
to glorify God
of disciplinary
least initially. It
the exposure and
Disciplinary autho
ple, to tell them tha
ing or doing. It is to
account of their error
correct their views a
properly applied, is lov
love, which knows that
willing to hurt.

Disciplinary authority is not
ministry of law and Gospel. It i
service of the Gospel. We are
and errors so that they will be
ing, illuminating, transformin
disciplinary authority, the ch
a patient into reality with a
that the patient will accept t

Relation to the Office of the

There is no term in Sc
what is here called discip
the disciplinary process a
lated are described in th
term employed here atte
concept. The Confessio
of "the power of jurisdi
excommunicate those w
them if they are conve
offenses may be either
authority "judge doc
to the Gospel, and e
whose wicked condu
excluded as well as
sake wicked teacher
of Christ, but are an

The power of j
plinary authority,
the Keys." Luther
given to the chur
to forgive sins a
primarily the c
and frequently
the Gospel.[6] H
law and judgm
sion of sin.[7]
which the Co
tive dimensi

labeled evangelical authority, the Confessors call "the power of order."[8]

It may be misleading to refer to the power of order as the positive or Gospel dimension of the keys and the power of jurisdiction as the negative or law dimension. Actually both dimensions contain both elements. However, the emphasis is different. The power of order, or evangelical authority, always includes the right and duty also to proclaim the law. And, the power of jurisdiction, or disciplinary authority, always includes the right and duty to proclaim the Gospel, to absolve those who repent. Order is primarily Gospel, and jurisdiction primarily law. In any case, it is interesting to note that the Confessions unite in a single concept two aspects of church authority which we have chosen to consider separately. These need to be seen in their unity. As has been mentioned previously, the several kinds of church authority discussed in this book are not separate or even only related entities. They are terms which refer to different aspects of the one authority which Christ has given to His people, the authority to proclaim the Gospel. For purposes of analysis it may be useful to distinguish among them, but, in reality, they are inseparably united.

A Continuum

Disciplinary authority may be regarded as a continuum. It is the spectrum of the church's response to those who have fallen into error, sin, or negligence. The response differs according to the condition of the offender. To the person who falls out of weakness or ignorance, the response is gentle. To the person who is more deeply or intentionally involved, or who refuses the gentle approach, a more severe response is necessary. To the person whose impenitence regarding error, sin, or negligence has severed him or her from Christ, the most drastic disciplinary measures are necessary. In some cases, the church is dealing with erring or straying Christians. In other cases it is dealing with former Christians, apostates. As we move across the scale from weak or erring Christians to apostates, the law element in the church's disciplinary expressions becomes increasingly prominent.

New Testament on Disciplinary Authority

1. *Admonition*[9]

According to the New Testament Christians have the right and the duty to admonish one another, to warn one another about error, sin, and negligence which have taken hold or which are threatening to do so. To admonish may be regarded as the mildest expression of disciplinary authority. It is the kind of help that every Christian needs constantly because the power of sin, though curtailed, continues to function even after the guilt of sin has been pardoned. Christians know from God's law that they are vulnerable to evil of every kind, that they make mistakes and are inclined to do what is wrong, often without realizing it. So, they are commanded to "teach and admonish one another" (Col. 3:16). This is done through apostolic leaders such as Paul (Acts 20:31; 1 Cor. 4:14), through other leaders (1 Thess. 5:12), as well as by means of the informal interaction of Christians with one another (Rom. 15:14; 1 Thess. 5:14). Essentially, this is the ongoing application of the law from Christian to Christian.

Although warning and condemnation of sin, error, or negligence is explicit, it is also done with the full recognition of the saving faith that remains in the person who is admonished. Admonition and warning is the act of a Christian brother or sister to another Christian brother or sister (Rom. 15;14; 1 Cor. 4:14; 2 Thess. 3:15). Moreover, admonition is a form of Christian concern whereby one approaches the weak or fallen person with the full realization of his or her own frailty, fallibility, and guilt. In the process of admonition, Christians relate to one another as fellow-sinners as well as fellow-redeemed. There is no room here for the admonisher to feel or act superior to the admonished. The purpose of admonition as well as every other exercise of disciplinary authority in the church is to restore the endangered person (Gal. 6:1-3). Thus, it is never merely a word of law, but also a declaration of the Gospel. It includes the "whole counsel of God" (Acts 20:27). It is a matter of letting "the *word of Christ* dwell in you richly" (Col. 3:16), which is, above all, a word of grace and forgiveness.

Various influences combine to make Christians reluctant to exercise the disciplinary authority of the church. From our pluralistic society we learn to tolerate a wide variety of ethical and theological views. We are prevented from imposing our beliefs and values on others, which is as it should be. An assumption that goes with this in the minds of many people and which may also affect the outlook of Christians even without their realizing it, however, is that there is no such thing as right and wrong, truth and error. There are only personal opinions and preferences. Whatever a person does or says, even if that person is one's fellow Christian, is strictly his or her own business. One has no right to interfere. He must not be judgmental. These relativistic assumptions, together with insufficient regard for God's Word, will inhibit Christians from giving admonition even where it is needed.

Obviously, there are also instances of admonition and other forms of disciplinary authority being over-used or given in a harsh, loveless, or self-righteous manner, and this is no better. What the New Testament calls for is discipline prompted by sincere concern for the faltering brother or sister based on knowledge of and confidence in God's revealed truth, and characterized by patience and sensitivity. Especially from the example of St. Paul in the Corinthian correspondence, we learn that the Christian must be willing to become involved and even to be misunderstood and rejected as he or she carries out the important responsibility and privilege of disciplinary authority.

2. *Censure*[10]

In the case of the Christian whose error, sin, or negligence is more serious and obvious, a response stronger than admonition is required. Such a person should receive what may be called "censure." That is to say, his or her fellow Christian(s) should rebuke, reprove, speak out in disapproval of the wrong. The person should be confronted with what is amiss in his or her doctrine or life. In some cases, for example, where the sin is a personal and private offense, the offender should be initially confronted in private. "Tell him his fault (censure) between you and him alone" (Matt. 18:15). If this is not effective, others should be involved in the confrontation. The purpose of the censure is not to punish the offender, but to gain him or her by inducing contrition (sorrow for sin) through the law and faith through the Gospel, which is always to be offered to the person who responds to the law with penitence.

If the offense is persistent and public, the censure should be public, that is to say, in the Christian assembly: "As for those who persist in sin rebuke (censure) them in the presence of all, so that all may stand in fear" (1 Tim. 5:20). This passage indicates the value of public censure not only to the offender, but also to others who might be inclined to deviate in a similar manner. Public censure by the church which is, in fact, the proclamation of God's own censure, the law, identifies right and wrong in a certain area of teaching or conduct, and expresses God's wrath and judgment against the wrong. Christian leaders have a special responsibility to censure: ". . . he (bishop) must hold firm to the sure word as taught, so that he may be able to give instruction in sound doctrine and also to confute (censure) those who contradict it" (Tit. 1:9; see also 1:13, 2:15; and 2 Tim. 4:2). However, censure is not the responsibility and prerogative only of leaders. All Christians possess it and should exercise it (Matt. 18:15; Eph. 5:11).

In the contemporary church there is an aversion to censure even more pronounced than the aversion to admonition mentioned above, and for the same reasons. We are too polite or too timid or too tolerant to censure each other, even when the spiritual welfare of the offender requires this. Reinforcing this aversion are the irresponsible, unjust, and cruel accusations made by a few. For example, publications which specialize in attack upon the theological and ethical positions of others, which consistently put the worst construction on everything, and which agitate for heresy trials and ecclesiastical purge, make all censure seem odious.

3. *Isolation*

The ultimate expression of disciplinary authority, short of excommunication, is the isolation of the offender from the Christian community. There are several instances in the New Testament in which St. Paul calls for this. It is not the same as excommunication, for the person is still regarded as a Christian. Is it a foretaste of excommunication, a sample of what will happen unless the person repents? Perhaps so.

> I wrote to you in my letter not to associate with immoral men; not at all meaning the immoral of this world or the greedy and robbers or idolators since then you would need to go out of the world. But, rather, *I wrote to you not to associate with anyone who bears the name of brother if he is guilty of immorality or greed, or is an idolater, reviler, drunkard, or robber—not even to eat with such a one* (1 Cor. 5:9-11 emphasis added).

> If any one refuses to obey what we say in this letter, note that man, and *have nothing to do with him*, that he may be ashamed. Do not look on him as an enemy but *warn him as a brother* (2 Thess. 3:14 emphasis added).

These references appear to apply to individuals who are guilty of gross public sins or errors, and who have not responded to the milder forms of disciplinary authority. Christian concern for them escalates. Measures to bring them to repentance intensify. Their unwillingness to respond to the spoken word of law makes it necessary to use what may be called a law action. The Christian community is to disassociate itself temporarily from the offenders, refuse to socialize with them, and, probably, refuse them the sacrament. This is to be done not in arrogance or self-righteousness, but in love in order to testify emphatically to the impenitence which the offenders are displaying, impenitence which could cut them off from God and His grace as well as from His people. The hope is that this law action will produce sorrow for sin, so that the Gospel can do its reconciling and transforming work. Although the faith of such offenders is regarded as terribly weak and seriously threatened, the assumption is that it remains to some degree, that the person is still in some sense a Christian.

4. *Exclusion*

Should isolation prove ineffective the next and strongest measure of disciplinary authority must be used, that reserved for those no longer regarded as Christians. The person must be excluded from the Christian community. He or she must be excommunicated. Neither "exclusion" nor its synonym "excommunication" are biblical terms. They are, however, convenient and adequate designations of what the New Testament describes and prescribes. ". . . if he refuses to listen to the church (i.e., to its admonition and censure) let him be to you as a Gentile and a tax collector" (Matt. 18:17) is the word of Jesus on this matter. Regarding the man who is living sinfully with his father's wife, for instance, St. Paul says, "Let him who has done this be removed from among you" (1 Cor. 5:2), and, "you are to deliver this man to Satan for the destruction of his flesh" (1 Cor. 5:5). In the case of a person who is splitting up the congregation over stupid and useless disputes, Paul says: "As for a man who is factious, after admonishing him once or twice, have nothing more to do with him, know that such a person is perverted and sinful; he is self-condemned" (Tit. 3:10).

Implied clearly in all of these cases is impenitence. The persons involved have refused persistently to heed the church's warnings and rebukes. They have been deaf to God's law as addressed to them through His people. They do not reject and repudiate their sin or error, but rather abandon themselves to it. In such a state they can not possibly receive or retain God's grace in the Gospel. Faith is dead. They are apart from Christ and under God's wrath. And, it is important that they be made fully aware of this. The church must announce with all emphasis that the bond with Christ and with them is completely broken, that they are no Christians, that they are condemned—not because they have sinned or erred, but because they are impenitent, not sorry for the wrong, but clinging to it. The purpose of this most drastic expression of disciplinary authority is the same as the less severe forms applied to those who are still Christians, namely, to evoke contrition, that sorrow for sin which prepares for the pardoning and restoring ministry of the Gospel: ". . .deliver this man to Satan for the destruction of the flesh, *that his spirit may be saved in the day of Jesus Christ*" (1 Cor. 5:5 emphasis added).

Confessions on Disciplinary Authority

1. *Similar to New Testament*

The Lutheran confessors do not use the term "disciplinary authority," nor do they organize the discussion of these matters as was done above. However, both the substance and the emphasis are similar. In the Confessions we have not only practical examples, but also a theological rationale for the application of God's law to the Christian. The former can be illustrated from practically every page of Luther's Large Catechism. Not only in the explanation of the Decalogue but in his treatment of the Creed and the sacraments, the Reformer admonishes and censures his readers regarding their incorrect views and sinful actions. His original readers were primarily pastors and preachers, many of whom were poorly-trained and ill-behaved. His purpose was not only to inform them, but to bring them to contrition, faith, and amendment of life and doctrine. In addition, he wanted to show them how to do the same for others.[11] The Formula of Concord explains why the Christian continues to need the ministry of God's law:

> But in this life Christians are not renewed perfectly and completely. For although their sins are covered up through the perfect obedience of Christ, so that they are not reckoned to believers for damnation, and although the Holy Spirit has begun the mortification of the Old Adam and their renewal in the spirit of their minds, nevertheless the Old Adam still clings to their nature and to all its internal and external powers. . . Hence, because of the desires of the flesh the truly believing, elect, and reborn children of God require in this life

> not only the daily teaching and admonition, warning threatening of the law, but frequently the punishment of the law as well, to egg them on so that they follow the Spirit of God.[12]

In his discussion of the Eighth Commandment Luther refers to the procedure commanded by Jesus in Matthew 18 for dealing with a fellow Christian who has sinned. He stresses the constructive purpose of these disciplinary actions—they are to try to help and improve the fallen person. When the disciplinary actions must become public, they also serve to alert and warn others against these errors and sins. Luther describes the increasing intensity of the action, from what we have called admonition, to rebuke, and, ultimately, to excommunication by an ecclesiastical court, if that should prove necessary. In all of this, those dealing with the offender should be scrupulously fair, and take every precaution against violating the person's rights and reputation.[13]

The only disciplinary step not covered by Luther in this connection is what we have called isolation, temporary disassociation from the impenitent Christian. The reason for this is that along with the other Confessors Luther does not appear to distinguish between the church's dealing with an impenitent Christian and its dealing with one whose impenitence has severed him or her from Christ. Both actions are called excommunication, because both involve refusing the sacrament to the person: ". . .excommunication excludes those who are manifest and impenitent sinners from the sacraments and other fellowship of the church until they mend their ways and avoid sin."[14]

2. *Purpose of Disciplinary Authority*

The primary purpose of disciplinary authority, as has been explained above in several places, is to help the person who has fallen into error or sin. Christians exercise this authority in its various forms in order to try to restore those who have fallen. In addition to this primary purpose and concern, there is also the intention to caution the rest of the church regarding the dangers to which some have fallen prey. This purpose remains secondary and subordinate to the first. In this section we point to something that is *not* a purpose of disciplinary authority, and that is the purification of the church.

Among the recurring heresies in Christendom is the notion that already in this world by the exercise of disciplinary measures the church must remove from its fellowship all serious sinners and errorists, that the validity and efficacy of the church's ministry are nullified by the presence of wicked people in it. The Donatists and Novatians in the early church, the Anabaptists of the Reformation Era, and Holiness Churches in modern times are examples of adherents of this view. The Lutheran Confessions, however, explicitly reject this view and the practices to which it leads:

> . . . we added the eighth article (of the Augsburg Confession) to avoid the impression that we separate evil men and hypocrites from the outward fellowship of the church or deny efficacy to sacraments which evil men or hypocrites administer. . . We concede that in this life hypocrites and evil men are mingled with the church and are members of the church according to the outward association of the church's marks—that is the word, confession, and sacraments—especially if they have not been excommunicated.[15]

This does not mean that the church, the kingdom and body of Christ, the assembly of those who share the same Gospel and the same Spirit, includes the wicked as well as the believing righteous. No, in the strict sense of the term "church" includes only true believers. Yet, in its outward appearance, in its external organizational manifestations, such disobedient and apostate people will always be found. The church is hidden under a crowd of wicked men, and yet its presence is revealed by the pure preaching of the Gospel and the sacraments.[16] We may and must distinguish between "the church properly so called" and "the church in the larger sense," which includes the wicked as well as the godly. However,

> This distinction between the real church and the outward fellowship of the church is a conceptual distinction of faith and hope but *not an empirical distinction to be realized concretely.* The latter would be the human anticipation of Christ's return. *The church must not separate saints from all sinners, but sanctify the sinners through the Gospel.*[17] (emphasis added)

Only at the Last Judgment will there be a complete and final separation between true and false Christians. In the meantime Christians are *not* to try to accomplish this with the exercise of disciplinary authority. Rather, they are to use this authority to try to salvage those who have become the casualties of sin and error, and to prevent other Christians from becoming such casualties.

3. *Grounds for Exclusion*

Exclusion is the most drastic form of the church's disciplinary authority, and it is to be employed only in those cases which clearly require it. Exclusion or excommunication, as already indicated, is the declaration of God through the church that the offender is apart from Christ and grace. It is the declaration that he is not forgiven, under divine judgment, and no longer a member of the church. To whom must the church make such a devastating declaration? What kinds of persons must be excluded? The Confessions identify three classes.[18]

The first is *those who persistently teach false doctrine which destroys the Gospel.* The criteria are clear: a radical threat to the foundation of faith, the Gospel, and an unwillingness to be corrected. Not everyone who errs on any doctrinal point, but rather the person whose error goes right to the heart of the matter, and who stubbornly insists on trying to gain adherents for the error, is to be excluded. Some errorists do not pose such a threat.

> Of course, there are also many weak people in it (the church) who build on this foundation (the true knowledge of Christ and faith) perishing structures of stubble, that is, unprofitable opinion. But because they do not overthrow the foundation they are to be forgiven and even corrected.[19]

Only those who overthrow the foundation by denying the central article of justification are to be excluded.[20] Excommunication is an action taken only against one who is no longer a Christian, whose error or disobedience is so profound and whose attitude so impenitent that faith has been destroyed. A person may adhere to and promulgate serious error which detracts from the Gospel. Yet, if that error does not destroy faith in the Gospel, that person should not be excommunicated.

That does not mean that nothing may be done about such false teachers. They must, of course, be admonished, censured, refuted, and, if necessary, isolated. All of these actions, including the last-mentioned, are short of excommunication, for all continue to recognize the offender as a Christian. There are references in the Confessions which appear to describe excommunication, but which on careful examination probably describe what I have called isolation.

The cases to which I refer are those of the Lutheran Theologians whose views are rejected in the Formula of Concord. These men erred seriously in doctrines related to the Gospel. They subbornly clung to and advocated these errors. However, in many cases their errors were not totally destructive of the Gospel, and they themselves continued to trust the Gospel although in a distorted and defective form. In other words, they were still the fellow Christians of the Confessors and not enemies of the Gospel or antichrists. Still, the Confessors condemned them and their doctrines very sharply and disassociated with them in a radical manner.

> We . . . specifically condemn . . . false and seductive doctrines and their stiff-necked proponents. These we do not by any means intend to tolerate in our lands, churches, and schools inasmuch as such teachings are contrary to the expressed Word of God and cannot coexist with it.[21]

Similarly the Formula itself states that "the opinions of the erring party cannot be tolerated in the church of God."[22]

Refusal to tolerate these theologians in the Confessors' lands, churches, and schools may sound like excommunication. However, in the light of their historical situation it appears to be more like what we would call suspension from office and/or suspension of church fellowship. Theirs was a religiously monistic society, rather than a pluralistic society such as ours. People of nearly all points of view agreed that to have more than one religion in a state or community would be productive of chaos and, therefore, intolerable. All dissenters from the official religion of a state or community were required to leave. Such a ban did not necessarily declare the person to be a non-Christian. It might simply mean that his or her error was serious enough to make worship and work together with that person impossible. The separation, in other words, was organizational rather than spiritual. It did not imply severance from the Body of Christ. In our pluralistic society the suspended false teacher could simply affiliate with a different Christian denomination. In the Reformation and Post-Reformation eras, however, since the boundaries of the external church and society were the same, organizational separation also involved banishment from the society.[23]

These observations lead to a contemporary application, some analysis and opinion for the reader's consideration. None of the resolutions or actions of the Missouri Synod in the current controversy are forms of excommunication. The persons most directly involved, the faculty majority of Concordia Seminary, St. Louis, were never judged to be advocates of errors which destroy the Gospel. They were never regarded as people who had departed from Christ. In fact, their clear profession of and commitment to the

Gospel were gratefully acknowledged. However, the Synod by convention action did repudiate an attitude toward the authority and clarity of Scripture perceived to be that of the faculty majority, an attitude "which reduces to theological opinion or exegetical questions matters which are, in fact, clearly taught in Scripture."[24] Examples mentioned in the Convention Proceedings are the facticity of miracle accounts, the historicity of Adam and Eve, the historicity of every detail of the scriptural account of Jesus, predictive Old Testament messianic prophecies, etc.

The key New Orleans Resolution 3-09 is clearly, first of all, an exercise of confessional authority (Chapter III). In it the majority of the delegates bear witness to the scriptural Gospel over against views which they believe threaten and undermine that Gospel. Furthermore, this resolution was also an exercise of organizational authority (Chapter V). In it members of the Synod were acting collectively according to agreed upon procedures, making decisions, and directing the responsible agency, the Board of Control of Concordia Seminary, St. Louis, to deal with the situation. Some argue, however, that the actions taken were *not* according to agreed upon procedures. The minority maintained that by reopening the case after a previous Board of Control had dismissed these charges, the Synod was, in fact, violating its own constitution.

Disciplinary authority was also prominent in the resolution. The Introduction of the New Orleans resolution referred to attempts to admonish and censure the faculty majority's position on certain points specifically by means of *A Statement of Scriptural and Confessional Principles* and the *Report of the Synodical President* based on the work of his Fact-Finding Commission. The terms "admonish" and "censure" were not used, but this was clearly the intended purpose of these documents. The president acting for the Synod was trying to warn and speak out against those whose doctrine was regarded as seriously deviant from Scripture and its Gospel norm, and thus in violation of Article II of the Constitution. The Introduction as well as the third "whereas" reported the faculty majority's refusal to accept the admonition and censure. It also reported the faculty majority's counter-charge that the theology expressed in the presidential documents was wanting. Intensified confessional and disciplinary measures followed in the third "resolved:"

> *Resolved,* that the Synod recognize that the matters referred to in the second resolved are in fact false doctrines running counter to the Holy Scriptures, the Lutheran Confessions, and the synodical stance and for that reason "cannot be tolerated in the church of God, much less be excused and defended" (FC, SD, Preface 9).[25]

If the analysis of this resolution and of similar statements in the Formula of Concord and the Preface to the Book of Concord given above is correct, the form of disciplinary authority referred to in the resolution is not excommunication but instead removal from office and possible termination of church fellowship. This, obviously, is strong discipline. However, it is much less than the ultimate step of excommunication.

Not everyone agrees with Synod's theological appraisal of the faculty majority's views on the controverted points. If the facts warrant it, and if that appraisal was arrived at sincerely and responsibly, the resolution would seem appropriate. In this instance, having concluded on the basis of its study and investigation that false doctrine was being taught, the Synod exercised disciplinary authority with increasing intensity. This was combined with confessional actions, and implemented through organizational actions. Those who believe that no false doctrine was being taught, of course, regard the actions as unwarranted, offensive, and oppressive.

The point here is that when Christians are convinced that serious and dangerous errors are being taught they have not only the right but also the duty, to act, to move across the spectrum of disciplinary authority as far as is necessary. Those who are charged with error also have the right to defend themselves and to appeal, if they regard the charges as inaccurate or unjust.

The second class of persons who must be excluded from the church are *manifest and impenitent sinners*.[26] Not all sinners are to be excluded. If they were, the church would not exist in this world. For all members, even the most devout and upright, continue to be corrupt in heart and life. Only *manifest* sinners are to be excluded, those whose sins are both gross and evident. Not secret sins or minor sins of weakness or ignorance, but open wickedness[27] and public offenses[28] call for the extreme disciplinary measure. Furthermore, only *impenitent* sinners should be excluded, those who refuse to respond to God's law as communicated in the admonition, censure, and isolation measures attempted by the church—those who persist in their sins despite the efforts of their fellow Christians to rescue them. Those, however, who respond to the church's discipline with contrition, sorrow for their sins, are to be absolved, regardless of the seriousness and notoriousness of their offenses.[29] In all of this it is important to recognize that the necessity for excluding the sinner is not based on the sin(s) or even the openness and gravity of the sin(s), but rather on the impenitence which these reveal. Not sin, but impenitence cuts a person off from Christ. The person who, instead of regretting and fearing sin, enjoys it and clings to it can not be forgiven and, therefore, can not belong to Christ. Manifest and impenitent sin represents a rejection of the Gospel. It violates and denies the Gospel just as effectively as does false doctrine.[30]

A third class of persons whom the church must exclude are *despisers of the sacraments:* "The openly wicked *and the despisers of the sacraments* are excommunicated."[31] Even more specific is Luther's statement in the Large Catechism: "Nevertheless let it be understood that people who abstain and absent themselves from the sacrament over a long period of time are not to be considered Christians."[32] Although the duty of excommunicating such persons is not explicitly mentioned in this connection, it is certainly implied. The reason why despisers of the sacraments are to be excluded is explained in the Reformer's discussion of confession—the vital element of which (the Gospel) is identical with that of the Lord's Supper:

> However, if you despise it and proudly stay away from confession, then we must come to the conclusion that you are no Christian and that you ought not receive the sacrament. For you despise what no Christian ought to despise, and you show thereby that you can have no forgiveness of sin. And this is a sure sign that you also despise the Gospel.[33]

The principle behind these statements is that to despise the medium of the Gospel is to despise the Gospel itself. Those who, because they care nothing for God's mercy in Christ, refuse to participate in the Lord's Supper or confession reveal their separation from Christ. Therefore, in their own best interests the church must call this separation and its consequences to their attention in the most forceful way possible. That is to say, they must be excommunicated.

It should be noted, though, that not everyone who abstains from the sacrament or confession is necessarily a despiser of the Gospel. People may abstain either because they are misinformed about these media of the Gospel, or because they are afraid that they do not qualify for participation, or because they have been refused admission, or because of neurotic inhibitions. Such persons, if they profess faith in the Gospel, should not be excluded but patiently instructed and encouraged. Only those whose absence from these Gospel media (the preaching and teaching of the Word included) because of contempt for the Gospel must receive this ultimate expression of the church's disciplinary authority.

Obedience to Disciplinary Authority

How are we to respond when our fellow Christians exercise disciplinary authority over against us? All of us are objects of that authority at one level or another. When because of our failures, misdeeds, errors, or negligence the church speaks a word of admonition or censure or even isolation or exclusion, how should this affect us? The answer becomes most apparent if the question is put into its basic form: When God speaks His Word of law to us how are we to respond? The exercise of disciplinary authority in the church is primarily the ministry of God's law. Obedience to disciplinary authority is the appropriate response to God's law, the response which He both intends and evokes through that law.

As with the obedience to every other kind of authority, obedience to disciplinary authority begins with hearing, listening, giving one's attention and consideration to the message with which one is confronted. In the case of the message expressed in an exercise of disciplinary authority, obedience means to hear what is said by human agents as God's own message of admonition, censure, or exclusion. It means to discern God's own authority in the bad news about one's self which the representatives of the church have announced. This simple aspect of obedience is easy enough to understand and, in theory, to accept. When faced personally in a concrete way with the judgments of God's law as interpreted by other human beings, however, we most often tend to tune them out or turn them off, or even to bristle in an angry and defensive manner and to respond with counter-charges and accusations. In short, obedience falters badly at this initial step. Regardless of one's position on the theological spectrum, regardless of one's ecclesiastical-political alignment, there is deep and powerful resistance to God Word of judgment when it gets close to the target. Too often the whole process breaks down for us right here. We may not be helped by the disciplinary authority of the church simply because we do not listen and take seriously what is said.[34]

This point is critical because this is a part of the process over which we have a significant measure of control. Only God's Word of law and Gospel can make the kinds of changes within us that are necessary for our justification and sanctification. However, that Word does not and can not work in us unless it gets past our ears and into our minds and hearts—unless we listen. We can not change our own hearts, but we can listen and thus receive the Word that can transform us. This is why Jesus in the Parable of the Sower emphasizes the importance of good listening: "He who has ears to hear, let him hear" (Mk. 4:9; Lk. 8:9). Even the person who is completely apart from Christ can make the decision to listen or not to listen:

> The person who is not yet converted to God can hear and read the Word externally because, as stated above, even after the Fall man still has something of a free will in these external matters, so that he can go to church, listen to the sermon, or not.[35]

If even the unregenerated have the power and freedom to listen to God's Word, how much more are we Christians, even in a state of sin or error, able to do this. Obedience to disciplinary authority begins with careful, attentive, humble listening.

The change that God wishes to make in us through His law and which by the Spirit He actually evokes, is called *contrition*. It consists, first of all, of recognition that we have disobeyed God's will and that we are corrupt beings. In the second place, it consists of remorse for that disobedience and for our inherent sinfulness, terrors of conscience, fear of God's wrath. Thirdly, it consists of repudiation, that is, rejection and renunciation of the evil that we are and do. To obey the disciplinary authority which conveys God's law to us in various ways is to be contrite, not to excuse our wrongs but to admit them and grieve over them and set ourselves against them. As our fellow Christians admonish, censure, or disassociate themselves from us, the response which God expects and enables is that we will be sorry for this evil, i.e., penitent. This is the second step of obedience to disciplinary authority.

The third step, the ultimate purpose of all disciplinary authority in the church is *faith*, in Christ, that we accept gratefully and confidently God's Word of pardon, that Gospel Word which is always offered to those who respond to the law with contrition. To obey disciplinary authority is to accept God's reconciling work in Christ and with that His rehabilitating work in the Spirit, that is, to accept both justification and sanctification.

The final stage of obedience to disciplinary authority is *amendment*, that we improve our behavior and/or correct our preaching and teaching so that they conform more closely to God's revealed will and truth. This step of amendment, like contrition and faith, is not one that we take out of our own resources, but by the power of the Holy Spirit conveyed to us through the Gospel.

In short, obedience to the disciplinary authority of the church is what the Confessions call repentance. Repentance equals contrition plus faith, and it implies amendment of life. This repentance is not a process that we go through only once at the time of conversion or occasionally at a time of recovery from an especially serious fall. Rather it is a process in which we are constantly engaged as God works in us through His law and His Gospel.[36]

Finally, it must be added, that obedience to disciplinary authority involves a willingness to exercise this kind of authority over others, to admonish, censure, and even to isolate and exclude those whose involvement in error, sin, or negligence require this. When we are the offenders, we must be willing to listen and repent. When others are the offenders, we must be willing to speak and act. This is our duty because it is commanded. It is also a privilege. For, our purpose in exercising this authority is not to hurt, but, to help, to restore and to gain the person who has fallen.

NOTES FOR CHAPTER IV

[1] Ap. XXVIII, 13 (Tappert, p. 283). See also Tr., 60 (Tappert, p. 330).
[2] A.C. XXVIII, 21 (Tappert, p. 80).
[3] Ap. VII and VIII, 48 (Tappert, p. 177).
[4] S.A. III, ix (Tappert, p. 314).
[5] Ap. XII, 176 (Tappert, p. 210).

[6] A.C. XXV, 4; XXVIII, 8 (Tappert pp. 62 and 82); Ap. XI, 2; XII, 39-43, 98-105 (Tappert, pp. 180, 187, 197); S.A. III, viii, 1-2 (Tappert, p. 312).

[7] A.C. XXVIII, 5 (Tappert, p. 81).

[8] Ap. XXVIII, 13 (Tappert, p. 283).

[9] All the passages cited in this section, except Gal. 6:1-3 use the Greek word νουθετειν This vocable as used in the New Testament conveys the idea of a gentle, evangelical effort to warn or instruct another about some threatening evil. It seems to assume inadvertent drifting toward the sin or error, rather than a fault of which the person is aware.

[10] The passages referred to in this section employ the Greek word ἐλεγχεῖν . As used in the New Testament this word expresses the idea of a more direct and severe encounter than νουθετεῖν one in which evil is exposed and condemned in no uncertain terms.

[11] L.C., Pref. (Tappert, pp. 358-365).

[12] F.C., S.D. VI, 7 and 9 (Tappert, p. 565).

[13] Tappert, pp. 402-403.

[14] S.A. III, ix (Tappert, p. 314).

[15] Ap. VII and VIII, 3 (Tappert, pp. 168-169).

[16] *Ibid.*, 19-20 (Tappert, p. 171).

[17] Edmund Schlink, *Theology of the Lutheran Confessions*, trans. by Paul F. Koehneke and Herbert J.A. Bouman (Philadelphia: Fortress Press, c. 1961), pp. 216-217.

[18] This section follows Schlink,*op.cit.*,pp. 211-215. However I stand issue with Schlink on one important point. See n. 23 below.

[19] Ap. VII and VIII, 20 (Tappert, pp. 171-172).

[20] *Ibid.*, 21 (Tappert, p. 172).

[21] Preface to *Book of Concord* (Tappert, p. 11).

[22] F.C., S.D. Antitheses, 15 (Tappert, pp. 506-507).

[23] Schlink p. 213 equates the action taken against the dissenting Lutheran theologians with excommunication. Edward W.A. Koehler, *A Summary of Christian Doctrine*, Second and Revised edition prepared for publication by Alfred W. Koehler (Oakland, Calif.: Alfred W. Koehler, c. 1952), p. 264 carefully distinguishes between denial of church fellowship and excommunication: "Denial of, or exclusion from, church fellowship is not the same as excommunication. While we may not tolerate the teaching and spread of false doctrine, it is possible that a person errs in sincerity of heart, without losing his faith in Christ (2 Thess. 3:14-15; 1 Cor. 3:11-15). We are to have no fellowship with false teachers (Rom. 16:17), yet we do not regard them as "heathen men and publicans."

[24] *Convention Proceedings, 50th Regular Convention The Lutheran Church—Missouri Synod New Orleans, Louisiana, July 6-13, 1973* Resolution 3-09, p. 139.

[25] *Ibid.*

[26] S.A. III, ix (Tappert, p. 314).

[27] Ap. XI, 4 (Tappert, p. 180).

[28] *Ibid.*, XXVIII, 13 (Tappert, p. 283).

[29] Tr., 60 (Tappert, p. 330); S.A. III, vii, and ix (Tappert, pp. 311 and 314).

[30] Schlink, *op. cit.*, pp. 213-214.

[31] Ap. XI, 4 (Tappert, pp. 180-181).

[32] L.C., Sac. Altar, 42 (Tappert, p. 451). See also S.C. Pref., 22 (Tappert, p. 451).

[33] L.C., Conf., 29 (Tappert, p. 460).

[34] "Of course, there remains also in the regenerated a resistance, of which the Scriptures say that the desires of the flesh are against the Spirit, and likewise that the passions of the flesh wage war against the soul, and the law in our members is at war with the law of our mind," F.C., S.D. II, 84 (Tappert, p. 537).

[35] *Ibid.*, 53 (Tappert, p. 531).

[36] For this section see especially Ap. IV and XII (Tappert, pp. 107-168; 183-211); S.A. III, iii, 1-9 (Tappert, pp. 303-304); and F.C., S.D. V (Tappert, pp. 558-563).

Disciplinary Authority

organizational
AUTHORITY

Chapter V

Organizational Authority

In order to communicate the Gospel effectively and extensively, and to do the confessional and disciplinary aspects of that task, God's people must organize. They must have assemblies and leaders, structures and plans, to facilitate the spread of the Gospel. The privilege and responsibility to proclaim the Gospel implies and includes the authority to organize for this purpose. Furthermore, there are explicit Scriptural precedents and directives which constitute a basis for organization and administration in the church. The very first Christians in Jerusalem immediately formed a worshipping and serving community under the leadership of the apostles (Acts 2:42-48). Soon leadership was expanded to include seven "deacons" (Acts 6:1-6) and elders (Acts 11:30).

When in Antioch of Syria many Gentiles as well as Jews were brought to faith in Jesus, they organized a church led by prophets and teachers and soon also became a missionary agency (Act 11:19-26, 13:1-3). As a result of Paul's work among the Gentiles not only were individuals converted, but also congregations were gathered and leaders appointed (Acts 14:20-28). Paul instructed a young associate to appoint leaders among the Christians of Crete (Tit. 1:5). Especially in the Pastoral Epistles (1 and 2 Tim. and Tit.), Paul gives detailed descriptions of qualifications for such leaders. The Epistle to the Hebrews urges Christians to remain involved and active in the assemblies in which they edified one another with the Gospel (Heb. 10:23-24). When controversy was provoked by the Judaizers, representatives of the Jewish and Gentile churches met in a council to make a collective decision (Acts 15).

The New Testament everywhere assumes and reflects organizational structure and persons functioning in leadership roles among the Christians. As they engaged in the organizational aspects of church life, Christians were not simply exercising an option or adopting a convenience. They were carrying out a privilege and responsibility which had been given to them. The Lord who had invested them with evangelical, confessional, and disciplinary authority had also given them the authority to organize for the purpose of carrying out this Gospel task. Speaking through the

Apostle Paul He commanded that all things in the church be done decently and in order (1 Cor. 14:40).

In this book the term "organizational authority" means the right and duty of Christians to organize so that they might coordinate their efforts to share the Good News. "Organizational authority" refers to matters of church polity or government, the regulation and management of the corporate activity of Christians. It has to do with designating people for leadership position, with response to that leadership, with the decision-making process of the church, and finally with programs, gathering and disbursing funds, and constitutional agreements. In this category belong questions about the relationship of individuals to the congregation, of the congregation to a larger collective, and of leaders and members to each other. Some of the most difficult and controversial issues troubling many church bodies today are aspects of organizational authority.

The term "organizational authority" is not found in the New Testament. It has been coined here in order to refer to those Scriptural precedents and injunctions mentioned above which indicate the will of Christ that His people organize under proper leadership to proclaim the Gospel, and that they go about this task in an orderly, effective manner. Nor is this term or its equivalent found in the Confessions. However, like the New Testament, the Confessions also describes the church as an ordered and directed entity. While the church is not merely or primarily an external organization and institution, it does have these features.[1] The church is led and served by ministers, bishops, pastors, and others who are selected by established and recognized procedures.[2] The church also has synods and councils to which the leaders are subordinate.[3] Through its leaders and governing bodies, regulations and rites may be initiated in the church in order to educate and guide the members and to avoid confusion.[4] Assuming that legitimate means are employed, all of this is as it should be. If God's people are to communicate the Gospel among themselves and to the world they must have leadership and organization. God wills that they have this. He authorizes them to establish and maintain it.

No Prescribed Form

The form of church organization is not divinely prescribed. The Lord who commissioned His people to evangelize, and who authorized them to organize for this purpose, did not specify any particular form that this organization should take. Few details are given in the New Testament about the organizational structure of the churches. However, what is stated suggests informal, fluid, and varied arrangements. As was mentioned above, at the beginning in Jerusalem the church was led by the apostles and their assistants. Within thirty years or less, non-apostolic leaders were in charge—James the brother of Jesus and the elders (Acts 21:18). In the churches that he founded or served, Paul acted as sort of a missionary bishop who gave counsel and instruction to local elders as well as directly to the congregations. Both the Acts narratives and Paul's letters reflect this. Some even believe that the references in Revelation to the "angels" (literally "messengers") of the seven churches (Rev. 1:20-3:22) are to human leaders rather than to celestial beings. In this case, we may have hints of a regional organization in which congregational leaders function in contact with one another under the supervision of an apostolic overseer.[5]

The New Testament Churches were organized. The form varied somewhat from place to place and even from time to time. Christians were not obligated to adopt a specific organizational pattern. Directed by the Spirit and their sanctified common sense, they adjusted their organizational forms to meet the needs of changing situations. The determining consideration was not simply convenience or personal preference, but rather what would best serve the Gospel. When the total leadership task became too much for the apostles, assistants were added. When the apostles were absent, these assistants were in charge. When decisions regarding the meaning and mission of the Gospel required collective consideration, they held a council. In other cases, individual leaders made the decision. Apparently, by the mid 50s the policy of remunerating church leaders was generally followed and was defended as divinely approved. However, when the proclamation of the Gospel was better served by a self-supporting ministry, that course was chosen. Virtually any adjustment was possible in the organization and ministry of the New Testament church, if the communication of the Gospel was thereby enhanced (1 Cor. 9).

The Confessions, too, leave the form of church organization unprescribed. The purpose and function are prescribed: to facilitate the proclamation of the Gospel. However, no binding statements are made about constitutions, style of government, and the like. Some passages assume an episcopal form of church government, in which the churches were ruled by bishops.[6] Others describe congregations acting with some autonomy.[7] That the church must have order and leadership is affirmed. How all this is arranged is a matter of Christian freedom, or, a matter of "human right."

This term, "human right," (*jus humanum*) is subject to misunderstanding. It does not refer to a natural right which Christians possess by virtue of their humanity. Rather, it is a privilege and responsibility bestowed upon them by God through the Gospel and for the Gospel. "Human right" means that God has given Christians the right to use their human judgment and ingenuity under the guidance of the Spirit to determine the manner in which the worship and work of the church should be organized.[8] If, for example, Christians wish to operate under a bishop and assign certain responsibilities such as ordination to him, they have that right. God has not stated that only bishops can ordain. Consequently, he does not have this authority by *divine* right. However, God has granted His people the option to make such an arrangement. If they do this, it is by *human* right that the bishop ordains.[9]

Similarly, liturgical calendars and ceremonies, and administrative regulations of all kinds are arrangements which Christians are free to make and to change. As they establish and modify ecclesiastical organization, Christians are to be guided by one overriding consideration: what will best enable them to carry out their Gospel commission?[10]

> Liberated by the Gospel for service to the Gospel "man" establishes ordinances in the church for examinations, ordinations, and installations, for the relationship of congregation, pastor, and church administrations for the unfolding of the functions of the *one* spiritual office in various offices arranged by the church, for the cooperation of the voice of the universal priesthood of believers in the activity of church administration, etc. . . Since even the New Testament statements concerning ecclesiastical order and its offices are not imposed as a law, but are received in the liberty of faith, the church is commanded to shout the Gospel into the world in ever-new advances, in ever-new forms and arrangements of the one spiritual office.[11]

This right and privilege to organize and reorganize for the cause of the Gospel, this freedom of Christians to determine what forms and regulations best aid the communication and celebration of the Gospel, must be preserved. No one should attribute a divine character to a humanly created ecclesiastical institution. No one should confuse human ordinances in the church with those which come from God Himself. Although human ordinances in the church are useful and may even be necessary, they must not be regarded as meritorious for salvation, nor sinful to disregard.

One aspect of Christian liberty is the freedom to make decisions in those matters neither commanded nor forbidden by God. This is the freedom to respond creatively to God's will and to the needs of others where God has left things open. Threats to and violations of this liberty are serious and numerous. Persons in positions of ecclesiastical leadership tend to equate their wishes with the will of God and their views with the truth of God. Like all human institutions, ecclesiastical institutions tend to resist even constructive criticism and to suppress necessary reform movements. Churchly traditions and practices in the course of time often become sacrasanct, and those who question or deviate from them may be regarded as heretics. A group of Christians may become so attached to their particular form of church government that they regard it as divinely ordained and denounce other forms as inferior or apostate. Affiliation with a certain congregation or church body is sometimes wrongly made a matter of conscience. In the face of all such threats Christian liberty must be affirmed.

That we organize to share the Gospel is required. *How* we do this is left to our discretion under the guidance of Word and Spirit. If a group of Christians is convinced that the Gospel is best served by a highly centralized form of church government, that is their privilege. If, for the same reason, they choose a less centralized or radically decentralized form, that is also their privilege. If a group of Christians feel that the Gospel is best served by disaffiliating with one church body and joining or forming another, that, too, is their God-given privilege and duty. Organizational authority is one aspect of the church authority possessed by all Christians. The element of freedom, which is an essential part of this authority, must be protected against every infringement.

Human Judgments

Decisions and regulations made by church leaders and governing assemblies are human judgments, finite and fallible. Although the Lord of the Church promises to guide His people by the Spirit as they deliberate and act in His name, He does not promise powers of omniscience or infallibility. As Luther observed, fathers, popes, and councils of the church have erred and contradicted each other, and, the Reformer himself makes many mistakes.[12]

Our regard for and reaction to churchly decrees must be tempered by this realization. On the one hand, we must trust the Spirit to work in and through His people. We must be open and sensitive to His direction in the decision-making processes of our church body. However, we must also be aware of our limitations and sinfulness individually and collectively. We must be willing to acknowledge and resist evil as it manifests itself in our ecclesiastical institutions as well as in our personal lives. A church body and its officials can be wrong, just as you and I or our respective congregations can be wrong. And yet, there are good reasons for taking the decisions of a church body very seriously and for deferring to its judgments and leadership.

> The obligation under which congregations consent to place themselves, to conform to the decision of synods, does not rest on any assumption that synods are infallible, but on the supposition that the decisions have been so guarded by wise constitutional provision as to create a higher probability of their being true and rightful than the decisions in conflict with them, which may be made by single congregations or individuals.[13]

The collective judgment of Christians, especially when this is arrived at very carefully, is more likely to be sound than that of an individual Christian or a single congregation.

At this point we are not referring to doctrinal and confessional decisions. These matters were considered in Chapter III. We are referring to the kinds of administrative and constitutional decisions by which a group of Christians endeavors to implement the proclamation of the Gospel.

Motivation

Motivation is a crucial consideration in every aspect of the church's life and work. Why we do something is at least as important as what we do. What should move Christians to exercise organizational authority in the church? Why whould we establish organizational units at various levels? Why should we make and implement corporate decisions? Everything that can be said about motivation in this connection can be reduced to faith and love (1 Jn.

3:23). Because we believe the Gospel and treasure it above all else, we work together to communicate it in the most extensive and intensive ways possible. Appreciation for the Gospel makes us willing to pool our resources with those of many other Christians. Regard for the One who is the Gospel leads us voluntarily, to limit our options and to accommodate ourselves to the wishes of others in certain respects, so that by our cooperative efforts we may project and magnify Christ on a larger scale than would otherwise be possible.

The other basic component of our motivation is love. Concern for others that they might receive the Gospel and its benefits moves us to organize. Hopefully, we will be able to reach more people with the Gospel and to reach them more effectively by larger cooperative efforts than by smaller or individual efforts. At least some things can apparently be done better by extensive and formal organization, such as training and placement of ministers, administration of a world mission program, work in the mass media, etc. Conscious of the needs of human beings for the Gospel and concerned to meet those needs, we organize. Faith and love are the reasons.

Or, at least, they should be. In reality our motives are always mixed and corrupt. Too often the driving force behind our organizational activities in the church are the desire for personal power and recognition, revenge upon our opponents, institutional idolatry or aggrandizement, pride, fear, insecurity, and the like. Only the process of repentance can deliver us from these unworthy motivational elements. Unfortunately, this process may be complicated and hampered by a situation in which several parties may be calling upon one another to repent, each firmly convinced that the wrong lies with the other(s). Ultimately, not man, but God, can evoke repentance. That is to say, only as God through the message of His law continually exposes and condemns these unworthy motives, can we recognize them for what they are, regret and repudiate them. Then, only as He ministers to us with the Good News of Christ can we receive pardon and the power to improve. Through His redemptive and rehabilitative Word, our unworthy motives can be counteracted and faith and love can be built up in their place.

Direction

In order to exercise organizational authority in a God-pleasing manner Christians also need proper direction. Even very highly motivated people will flounder if they lack clear and reliable guidance. In conducting the organizational activity of the church, Christians should be guided by Scriptural ethical norms and sanctified common sense. Some of the questions which we must decide in our church organizations are substantially or even primarily *moral* issues. For example, should we speak out or act with regard to world hunger, racism, or abortion? Should we initiate or discontinue fellowship with another church body? Should we censure or dismiss those who dissent from our organizational regulations? These are questions of right and wrong. They require us to determine what we believe God wants us to do and to avoid. For assistance in dealing with moral questions Christian organizations as well as individuals need to consult the Bible and be guided by its norms.

Not all questions faced by Christian organizations are primarily moral or even theological. Many are practical questions concerned with what course of institutional action is likely to be most effective, most economical, most advantageous in other ways. (Should we open, close, or relocate this college or seminary? Should we revise our organizational structure? Should we conduct our publishing enterprise in a different manner?) Questions of this kind are to be decided upon the basis of reason or common sense. God has not provided us with revealed directives for such decisions. He has equipped us with the ability to think, to analyze, to project, to solve problems. For direction and guidance in the practical matters of the church's life we are to rely upon reason—our own and that of others.

Obviously, few questions confronting church organizations are exclusively moral issues or exclusively practical matters. The moral questions usually have their practical aspects and *vice versa*. In most cases the study of biblical norms must be combined with rational reflection in order to decide what course of action should be taken. The very process of interpreting the Bible in order to discover its ethical principles is in part a rational exercise involving linguistic, historical, and cultural study.[14]

To say that Christians should be guided by Scripture and common sense as they function in their ecclesiastical organizations is simple enough. But, precisely what are the biblical ethical norms that we should follow? And what, in a given situation, is the most sensible and rational thing to do? Although some take an antinomian position, denying that the Bible gives us any binding moral guidelines, Lutheranism and most of historic Christianity affirm the existence and validity of such guidelines.[15]

There is not a clear consensus, however, as to what these norms are or how they apply to the issues which we confront. Basic are the Ten Commandments, but this is just the beginning. In addition, we find many other moral directives in the Bible, many of which may be regarded as commentaries on the commandments. There is the Sermon on the Mount (Matt. 5-7) and numerous passages in the epistles which describe and prescribe the kind of attitudes and behavior which God wills in those whom He has redeemed. Furthermore, there are moral examples, positive and negative in the Bible, and they are written for our instruction (Rom. 15; Heb. 11). There are the basic principles of love, truth, justice, and sanctity of human life expressed in various ways throughout Scripture. Above all, there is the person and work of Jesus Christ. From this assortment of biblical materials about attitudes and behavior, we are to form an impression, a vision, of what the Christian life is to be like. It is important to note that what Scripture provides is not a complete moral code, but a model. The composite of what Scripture says about right and wrong constitutes a sketch of a certain kind of person, a Christ-like person. Each command or direction is line or patch of color, a vital part of that sketch. Our decisions and actions are to conform to that model, whether we are functioning as Christian individuals or corporately. The model is clear and authoritative.[16]

The problem is that Christians often perceive and interpret the model differently. They disagree about what God commands and prohibits in Scripture, for example, on the ordination of women to the pastoral ministry. Or, in the case of conflicting principles or values, they disagree about which is to take priority. For example, is it right, out of concern for Christian truth, purity of doctrine, to force dissenting persons out of their ministries? Or, should we in Christian love be more tolerant of questionable theology?

Some insist that in the conflict between truth and love, love must yield. Or, they explain that it is lovelessness of the worst kind to tolerate false doctrine. Others maintain that a passion for truth that deals harshly with fellow Christians is fanaticism. Here we are drifting back into the subject matter of the earlier chapter on "Confessional Authority."

At this point we simply wish to note that sincere and informed Christians, even those committed to similar or identical theological perspectives, can not always agree what the moral direction of Scripture is in a given situation, i.e., what is right and what is wrong to do. Just as in practical matters, opinions may differ sharply on what course of action would be wisest and most promising. Certainly, this is a root problem in the exercise of organizational authority in the church: How to deal with disagreement, serious disagreement, about the morality and rationality of a certain course of action.

Obedience

Obedience, we have said, is the appropriate response to authority. The form of obedience will be determined by the nature of the authority to which it is responding. Organizational authority in the church is something unique. It is not a relation of superiors to inferiors, but rather an authority which exists among equals and is manifest as humble service (Matt. 23:10-12). The position advanced in this presentation is that obedience to organizational authority in the church takes the form of loving cooperation and faithfulness to agreements. The organizational leaders of the church at every level speak and act directly for God when they are in the process of proclaiming the Gospel Word. However, when they are in the process of deciding how best to go about that task, they are speaking and acting for and with their fellow Christians, fellow human beings who are their colleagues and associates, not their subordinates. Consequently, obedience to the organizational authority of the church is *not* something covered by the Fourth Commandment. Rather, it relates to the image of the church as the Body of Christ (1 Cor. 12; Eph. 4) and to the Great Commission (Matt. 28:20).

Christians are not isolated individuals. We are related organically to one another within the body of Christ. We are to function corporately and in a complementary manner. We are to work with and for each other as we reach out to the world with the Gospel.

We are gifted diversely with regard both to spiritual and natural abilities. And yet, these differences are not to be divisive, but supportive and unifying. Each member is designed to serve the others in some essential way, and all together are to honor God by the proclamation of the Gospel for the salvation of the lost (1 Cor. 12; Rom. 15:1-13). In order to worship and work together harmoniously and effectively, we must accept and respect one another. We are to be patient, selfless, considerate of others, and deferential to their wishes, tolerant of their weaknesses, and sensitive to their needs (Rom. 12, 14; 1 Cor. 13; Phil. 1:27-2:11).

Furthermore, we must accept or develop suitable procedures and policies both for worship and for work. There must be order in the church rather than anarchy. Once agreements and commitments have been made they should be honored, not out of constraint, but willingly and joyfully (Matt. 18:15-17; 1 Cor. 14, 16:1-4; 2 Cor. 9). Factions, cliques, and dissension in the corporate life of the church are violations of the Lord's will and an obstacle to the Gospel (Jn. 17:11-23; 1 Cor. 1:10-17, 3; Eph. 2:11-22, 4:1-6).

The Confessions, too, emphasize the necessity of loving cooperation with the organizational authority of the church.

> With regard to church usages that have been established by men, it is taught among us that those usages are to be observed which may be observed without sin and which contribute to peace and good order in the church, among them being certain holy days, festivals and the like. Yet we accompany these observances with instruction so that consciences may not be burdened by the notion that such things are necessary for salvation.[17]

We are to go along with these human arrangements and regulations, not because they justify, but because they are helpful.

> It is proper for the Christian assembly to keep such ordinances for the sake of love and peace, to be obedient to the bishops and parish ministers in such matters, and to observe the regulations in such a way that one does not give offense to another and so that there may be no disorder or unbecoming conduct in the church. However, consciences should not be burdened by contending that such things are necessary for salvation or that it is a sin to omit them even when no offense is given to others.[18]

Christian individuals and groups are to extend themselves to the utmost to comply with the regulations and policies of their church leaders and governing bodies. The only limit to obedience is that which violates God's own will. Such violations are regulations or interpretations of regulations which would undercut the Gospel or confuse human ordinances with ordinances of God, in which case consciences would be bound and Christian liberty violated. There is nothing here to encourage a spirit of autonomy or rebellion over against the ecclesiastical institution. Instead, it is a commitment to humble and loving cooperation. The Lutheran Confessions are not a proclamation of emancipation from the organizational authority of the church. Throughout their documents, the Confessors affirm their loyalty and obedience to that authority, qualified only in the manner that the Gospel requires.

> Moreover, we should not only obey the preaching but also the regulations which the church has adopted in the unity of faith and love for the preservation of preaching. . . Also disobedience to an ordinance of the church instituted by human right is disobedience to God since it violates the law of love.[19]

Disobedience

As has already been suggested, occasions do arise when it is right and necessary to disobey the organizational authority of the church. There are even occasions when church leaders and institutions must be repudiated. Already in the New Testament we have instances of this. In Antioch Paul felt compelled to oppose Peter's cowardly concessions to the Judaizers because these concessions gave the dangerously false impression that justification is at least in part by the works of the law (Gal. 2). Subsequently, in his letter to them Paul pleads with the Galatians to resist all leaders and practices which undercut the Gospel. Anyone who perverted the Gospel, regardless of the person's status, should be discredited and disobeyed. Even if Paul himself were to do this, or an angel from heaven, they would be under God's curse and should not be followed (Gal. 1:6-9). Note that in the instance of the Judaizers we are dealing not only with false teaching (which was the concern of Chapter III) but with regulations and practices which distort or deny the Gospel.

Elsewhere, Paul warned against those whom the Spirit said would depart from the faith, and try to lead others to do the same by imposing as necessary for salvation various ascetic practices (1 Tim. 4:1-5). Peter warned against leaders who would pervert the Gospel by making it license for immoral practices (2 Pet. 2). A similar reference is found in the letter of Jude. In Revelation John condemned Christians in Pergamum and Thyatira for not resisting those who were leading them into idolatrous and immoral practices (Rev. 2:12-29). In general, the New Testament commands disobedience to leaders, regulations, and practices which violate or deny the Gospel or the revealed will of God.

The Lutheran Confessors were in a situation which called for careful interpretation and application of these Scriptural principles. They were initially in a state of dissent from their ecclesiastical leaders and institution and, ultimately, separated from them. They were concerned in all of this to be directed by the Word of God. Essentially, their position is this: Church leaders and institutions must be disobeyed whenever they try to make anyone else teach or practice contrary to the Gospel.[20] All other directives and ordinances the Confessors would continue to follow.[21] Only those directives which are clearly anti-Gospel should be disregarded.

At what point and for what reasons must church leaders and organizations be totally repudiated? If they are guilty of hypocrisy or immorality? Not necessarily. God can work through the means of grace even if they are administered by wicked persons.[22] If they teach and practice contrary to the Gospel? Not necessarily, at least, not right away. At Augsburg (1530) and for sometime afterward, the Confessors did not insist as a condition for their remaining in the Roman Church that all anti-Gospel teaching and practice be eliminated. The Confessors simply insisted that *they* be permitted to teach and practice according to the Gospel. Actually, they hoped to remain in that imperfect organization and in communication with their erring and heavy-handed leaders in the hope of influencing them with the Gospel.[23]

What, then, constituted the basis, ultimately, for separation from these leaders and this ecclesiastical organization? The conviction that they were enemies of the Gospel who were attempting to prohibit preaching and practicing according to the Gospel. Already in the Smalcald Articles (1537) it is clear that Luther had come to this conclusion. Eventually most of his followers came to share that conclusion.[24] Not only did the Pope and his followers insist on continuing their anti-Gospel teaching and practices, but they were also determined to impose them by force on others. The Pope, Lutherans came to realize, was not only a false teacher, but actually an anti-Christ. In the judgment of these Lutherans, the center of Roman worship, the mass, and the most influential Roman institution, monasticism, were profoundly incompatible with and detrimental to the Gospel.[25]

The Difference Democracy Makes

As has been observed above, the form of obedience is determined by the type of authority to which it is responding. The organizational authority of the church will differ according to the type of church government which is in effect. No specific form of church government has been instituted by God. Christians are free to create, adapt, or adopt any form that will best serve the communication of the Gospel. They may adopt a highly centralized and authoritarian form, or, a decentralized and democratic form, or something in between. In an authoritarian form, the distinction between leaders and followers is very obvious. Some have the responsibilities of leaders, and others the responsibilities of followers. Obedience to organizational authority, where this form of church government is in effect, consists largely of taking orders.

In the case of a democratic form of church government, the situation is significantly different. Christians who belong to an organization with this form of government have responsibility to lead as well as to follow. Not only do they have the obligation to comply with the rules and to obey their leaders, but also they have the right and the duty to help make decisions, to establish policies and regulations, and to elect leaders. Furthermore, they have the responsibility to work for change where change is needed in order to accomplish the Gospel task more efficiently.

For any democratic organization to function properly, individuals and groups within it must have the opportunity to express themselves freely. They need the opportunity to influence the views of others in the organization. They must have the right to dissent from established views and policies.[26] Dissent within a democratic organization is not the same as disobedience. In effect, it may be an aspect of obedience to organizational authority. That is to say, it is a way for those within that organization to affect its course and character, which is their responsibility in a democracy. Dissent is compatible with compliance. One may cooperate with leaders and regulations with which he/she disagrees, and should do this, unless this would involve violation of God's will and Word. If freedom of expression is radically curtailed or if channels of dissent are inadequate, the democratic character of the organization is in jeopardy.

Level of Compliance

In order to function effectively and even to survive, the organizational structures of the church must require a certain level of compliance with their regulations. Profound and persistent noncompliance threatens the existence of the organization and thus the fulfillment of its purpose. Expression of this is given in the constitutions of most congregations and synods. There are various conditions of memberships, one of them usually being reasonable compliance with the provisions of the constitution.

While acknowledging the rights and freedoms of the members, constitutions also state the responsibilities of the members to the organization. Membership in the group implies substantial acceptance of its purposes, agreement with its policies, and support of its programs. The free decision to join the organization involves a pledge to cooperate with it. There is inevitably some tension between the rights and freedoms of the members and the decisions and requirements of the organization. Some non-compliance can safely be tolerated, especially in a voluntary organization, which is what virtually all ecclesiastical organizations are. If the level of non-compliance rises too high, however, and regard for the collective will falls too low, cooperative effort becomes extremely difficult and eventually impossible.

Analysis and Opinion Related to Current Questions

If these observations and opinions are valid, a church organization should not be condemned out of hand for attempting to secure compliance with its regulations. If the purpose of that organization is what it ought to be – the promulgation of the Gospel – and if that purpose is being faithfully carried out, the organization should struggle to survive, not for its own sake, but for the sake of the Gospel. It is not necessarily legalism or tyranny for an ecclesiastical organization to press its members to comply with the regulations which its governing body has drawn up. To the contrary, this may be a responsible effort to maintain and strengthen an instrument of the Gospel.

The vital and hard questions are: how high a level of non-compliance is too high? In which areas are non-compliance most threatening? And, how should a church organization deal with those whose non-compliance is judged intolerable? No complete or final answers are attempted, only some suggestions to stimulate thought and discussion. The reader is reminded that the kinds of non-compliance referred to in this chapter are not those that are primarily doctrinal. The earlier chapter on "Confessional Authority" dealt with that. Here we are discussing non-compliance with organizational regulations which, although they may have a doctrinal base or may ultimately serve a doctrinal purpose, are of themselves practical. Some examples of this type of regulation which figure prominently, for instance, in the Missouri Synod controversy are those which deal with the admission of unauthorized candidates to the ministry,[27] the relationship between district presidents and the synod,[28] and the relation of members of the synod to an association within its midst, such as Evangelical Lutherans in Mission.[29]

The level of non-compliance may be regarded as too high if a clear majority of the members is convinced that it is too high. This is a hypothesis offered for the reader's consideration. If a group of Christian individuals and congregations has been formed around the principle that all matters not determined by the Word of God are to be decided by majority vote,[30] this would seem for them to be the proper way to determine whether or not non-compliance has passed a tolerable level. The group, mindful of its purpose and what measures and arrangements best serve the fulfillment of that purpose, must assess the quantity, the quality, and the intensity of the resistance that some in the group are expressing. If, over a period of time after serious negotiation and reconsideration, the majority remains convinced that its chosen course must be pursued and that the level of non-compliance by dissenters is too high, it probably is. Like all human judgment, this kind may be erroneous. It would seem though, that no other party would be in a better position to determine the answer to this question than the majority. If non-compliance is permitted to continue and grow after a majority of the members is convinced that it is intolerable, chaos or even collapse of that organization would seem probable.

Non-compliance is most dangerous in those areas related to the central purpose of the organization. Since the training and supervision of ministers and teachers are among the basic objects of the Missouri Synod[31] it is not surprising that non-compliance with the three regulations mentioned above has been viewed with alarm. However well-intentioned and whatever the provocation, to train and ordain ministers for congregations of synod apart from and in competition with prescribed institutions and channels understandably appears dangerously subversive to many.

Every major Lutheran synod in America and, in fact, most Christian bodies, maintain firm control over the admission of candidates to their ministries. Although they may not all insist on training the candidates themselves in their own colleges and seminaries, the vast majority of denominations allow the admission only of those candidates approved by the designated agency of the general body. Throughout most of Christendom, attempts to bypass or to compete with established agencies of approval and admission to the ministry are regarded as intolerable and as organizational rebellion. That a congregation has the divine right to ordain ministers without approval of a general body is not questioned. The point is simply that in most ecclesiastical organizations congregations delegate this responsibility to the general body, and that most general bodies insist on this arrangement as a condition of membership.

Non-compliance also appears gravely menacing in those areas which involve the control and management of an organization. Can an organization afford to permit its officers to decline to carry out the considered and clearly stated will of the governing body or to operate in a matter inconsistent with its constitution? This appears to be the fundamental issue behind the resolutions and actions against some of the Missouri Synod district presidents who conducted unauthorized ordinations. From the perspective of personal courage and integrity, it may have been admirable for these district presidents to have followed conscience rather than synodical policies which they believed to be erroneous and unjust. From the perspective of the synod as an organization, however, it was failure to uphold constitutional responsibilities which, in turn, threatened the entire administrative operation of the synod. Would it have been responsible for the synod to permit people to continue in high leadership positions who refused to comply with some of its important regulations? Could the organization long survive that kind of non-compliance? Opinions differ sharply, of course. Those who agree with the district presidents in question believe that, instead of disciplining them, the synod should have heeded their protest and changed its ruling. Others, the majority of the convention delegates, were convinced that the organizational as well as the theological integrity of the synod required the ruling, that it was both just and necessary. It was a painful and tragic clash of consciences as well as a constitutional crisis.

How should an ecclesiastical organization deal with those whose non-compliance is judged intolerable? How should those who are compelled by conscience not to comply deal with the organization? With love, patience, honesty, and justice—all parties would agree on the principles. When it comes to applying these principles, the consensus disappears. Only one biblical precedent comes to mind and the parallel is by no means exact. At the beginning of his Second Missionary Journey, Paul and his co-worker Barnabas, who had accompanied him on the First Missionary Journey, had a serious disagreement on a practical matter of some importance. Barnabas, an exceptionally generous and supportive person, wanted to take along John Mark. Paul violently opposed the idea, because Mark had started out with them on the First Journey and then dropped out an an early point, apparently for no good reason. Barnabas wanted to give Mark another chance. Paul would not agree (Acts 15:36-41).

This, of course, is an incident between two individuals, rather than an organizational development. However, the essential factors seem similar. Two parties who had been cooperating experienced unresolvable conflict about how to go about the task of getting the Gospel out. Paul, who enjoyed the support of the Antioch congregation (majority?), chose a new partner, Silas, and went off on his journey as planned. Barnabas, apparently with little or no support from the Antioch congregation, took Mark and went in a different direction, to Cyprus, the scene of Mark's earlier defection. They separated, not spiritually, but organizationally, we might say. Since disagreement prevented their working together, they worked separately—at the same Gospel task. As far as we can tell there was no lasting bitterness over the disagreement or separation.

Two later references to Barnabas in Paul's correspondence contain nothing negative or disparaging about his former associate (1 Cor. 9:6; Col. 4:10).[32] That is not to suggest that this separation was painless. The relationship between Paul and Barnabas had been long and close. Barnabas was the one who, after Paul's conversion, persuaded the apostles at Jerusalem that Paul's conversion was authentic and that they should accept him as a brother and no longer be afraid or suspicious of him, their former persecutor (Acts 9:26-27). It was Barnabas who more than a decade later recruited Paul for ministry at Antioch where large numbers of Gentiles were being gathered into the church (Acts 11:19-26). It was Barnabas who shared Paul's dangers and joys on his First Missionary Journey (Acts 13 and 14) and who stood beside him at the Apostolic Council in Jerusalem contending for the rights of the Gentile Christians (Acts 15). A long and fruitful association dissolved over that disagreement concerning John Mark, but it dissolved peacefully and lovingly.

Organizational Separation

Is organizational separation an answer when parties within an ecclesiastical organization arrive at serious and irreconcilable differences over practical management of their organization? Apparently Paul and Barnabas came to that conclusion. Certainly, every effort should be made either to resolve the differences or to live with the differences. If the differences make cooperation impossible, then, perhaps, organizational separation is necessary and even wholesome.

Distinctions should be made between organizational separation, the disruption of church fellowship, and the fragmentation of the Body of Christ.

Church fellowship can be disrupted. When Christians disagree so seriously in doctrine that joint worship and work become a source of dissension, confusion, or a denial of the truth, then they ought to avoid worshipping and working together for the time being.

Organizational separation is something else again. It may amount simply to a recognition that divergent or conflicting views about how to do the Lord's work make it desirable or necessary for the parties in question to function independently. It is possible to be separate organizationally and yet be in pulpit and altar fellowship.

Almost from the beginning, the Lutheran Church-Missouri Synod, for instance, has related in this way to some other Lutheran bodies in this country and abroad, e.g., for nearly a century with members of the Synodical Conference and more recently with the American Lutheran Church. It is also possible that a church group, such as the Missouri Synod, could remain in fellowship with some of those who feel compelled to organize separately at this time, or at least could work toward such a fellowship in the future.

The fragmentation of the Body of Christ in its basic sense, of course, never really happens. The church is one and always will be: "There is one body and one Spirit. . .one Lord, one faith, one baptism, one God and Father of us all. . ." (Eph. 4:4-6). No matter what happens in the external life of the church, Christians are united with every other person who truly believes in Jesus, despite differences and disagreements, regardless of synodical and denominational affiliation. Nothing can disrupt this essential unity.

NOTES TO CHAPTER V

[1] Ap. VII and VIII, 1-15 (Tappert, pp. 168-170).

[2] A.C. V (Tappert, p. 31); Tr. 60-68 (Tappert, pp. 330-331).

[3] *Ibid.*, 49-59 (Tappert, pp. 328-330).

[4] A.C. XXVIII, 53-60 (Tappert, pp. 89-91); Ap. VII and VIII, 33 (Tappert, pp. 174-175).

[5] Henry Barclay Swete, *The Apocalypse of St. John: The Greek Text with Introduction Notes and Indices* (Grand Rapids, Mich.: Wm. B. Eerdmans Publishing Co., n.d.), pp. 21-22.

[6] A.C. XXVIII (Tappert, pp. 81-94), Ap. XXVIII (Tappert, pp. 281-285).

[7] S.A. III, x (Tappert, p. 314); Tr., 63-68 (Tappert, p. 331).

[8] Edmund Schlink, *Theology of the Lutheran Confessions*, translated by Paul F. Koehneke and Herbert J.A. Bouman (Philadelphia: Fortress Press, c. 1961), pp. 247-254.

[9] Tr., *ibid.*

[10] Ap. XXIV, 1-3, 38-49 (Tappert, pp. 249-250, 257-258); F.C., S.D., X (Tappert, pp. 610-616);see also Schlink, *ibid.*

[11] *Ibid.*, pp. 252-253.

[12] "On the Councils and the Church", trans. by Charles M. Jacobs rev. by Eric W. Gritsch, in *Luther's Works Vol. 41, Church and Ministry III*, ed. by Eric W. Gritsch, gen. ed. Helmut T. Lehmann (Philadelphia: Fortress Press, c. 1966), pp. 3-178.

[13] Charles Porterfield Krauth, quoted by Conrad Bergendoff, "The Authority of the Synod in Relation to the Authority of the Congregation—II", *American Lutheran* XIV, 29.

[14] See my *Reason and Religion* (Saint Louis: Concordia Publishing House, c. 1965).

t that the glory and power of the
dual and collective shortcomings.
not ourselves, but Jesus Christ as
his treasure in earthen vessels, *to*
er belongs to God and not to us,"

ospel, renews, restores, heals, and
h. The controversy about authori-
bout the Gospel. To the extent that
the Gospel and involves them in
e Gospel, it is potentially a source

[15] F.C., S.D. VI (Tappert, pp. 563-568). Prominent among those whose ethical approach virtually negates binding ethical norms from the Bible or any other source are Joseph Fletcher, *Situation Ethics* (Philadelphia: Westminister Press, c. 1966) and Paul Lehman, *Ethics in a Christian Context* (New York: Harper, c. 1963).

[16] The ability to conform, however, comes not from these ethical injunctions themselves but from the Gospel and from the Spirit who is mediated by the Gospel. There is also a sense in which the Spirit gives the Christian moral direction from within—enlightening and guiding the Christian through the difficult and uncertain moral decision which he/she often confronts. This direction does not conflict with the Scriptural injunctions, but rather aids their understanding and their application to situations not covered by biblical teaching.

[17] A.C. XV, 1-2 (Tappert, p. 36).

[18] *Ibid.*, XXVIII, 55-56 (Tappert, p. 90).

[19] Schlink, *op. cit.* pp. 256-257.

[20] A.C. *ibid.*, 23-28 (Tappert, pp. 84-85).

[21] *Ibid.*, 53-60 (Tappert, pp. 53-91).

[22] *Ibid.*, VIII (Tappert, p. 33).

[23] *Ibid.*, XXVIII, 71-72 (Tappert, p. 93). See also the concluding statement of the first part of the A.C. (Tappert, pp. 47-48) as well as A.C. XXVII, 76-78 (Tappert, p. 94). Basically, the entire Augsburg Confession is a plea for toleration within the Roman Church of evangelical preaching and practice.

[24] S.A. Pref., 15 (Tappert, p. 291).

[25] *Ibid.*, II, ii-iv (Tappert, pp. 293-301); Tr., 39-59 (Tappert, pp. 327-330).

[26] Reference here is not to dissent from the content of the Gospel message, but rather dissent from the way in which the organization goes about getting the message out. In other words, not doctrinal dissent, but dissent from regulative decisions.

[27] *Handbook of the Lutheran Church-Missouri Synod 1973 Edition,* Bylaw 4:19, pp. 98-99.

[28] *Convention Proceedings 51st Regular Convention The Lutheran Church-Missouri Synod, Anaheim, California, July 4-11, 1975.* Resolution 5-08 pp. 126-127.

[29] *Ibid.*, Resolution 3-06, pp. 96-99.

[30] *Handbook*, Constitution, Art. VIII, c., p. 18.

[31] *Ibid.*, Art. III, 3 and 7, pp. 15-16.

[32] If a late date is given to the Epistle to the Galatians there are three additional references to Barnabas after the separation (Ch. 2), also favorable. Incidentally, it would appear that Barnabas' judgment about John Mark was more accurate than that of Paul and the Antioch congregation. This young worker whom Barnabas salvaged after such an inauspicious beginning went on to become an associate of Peter and the author of the gospel which bears his name.

We can take comfort in the fa
Gospel can transcend our indivi
Fortunately, "what we preach is
Lord," (2 Cor. 4:5). "We have t
show that the transcendent pow
(2 Cor. 4:7 emphasis added).

Finally, this authority, this G
unifies all who confront it in fai
ty in the church is controversy a
this controversy draws people t
study of and reflection upon th
of tremendous blessing.

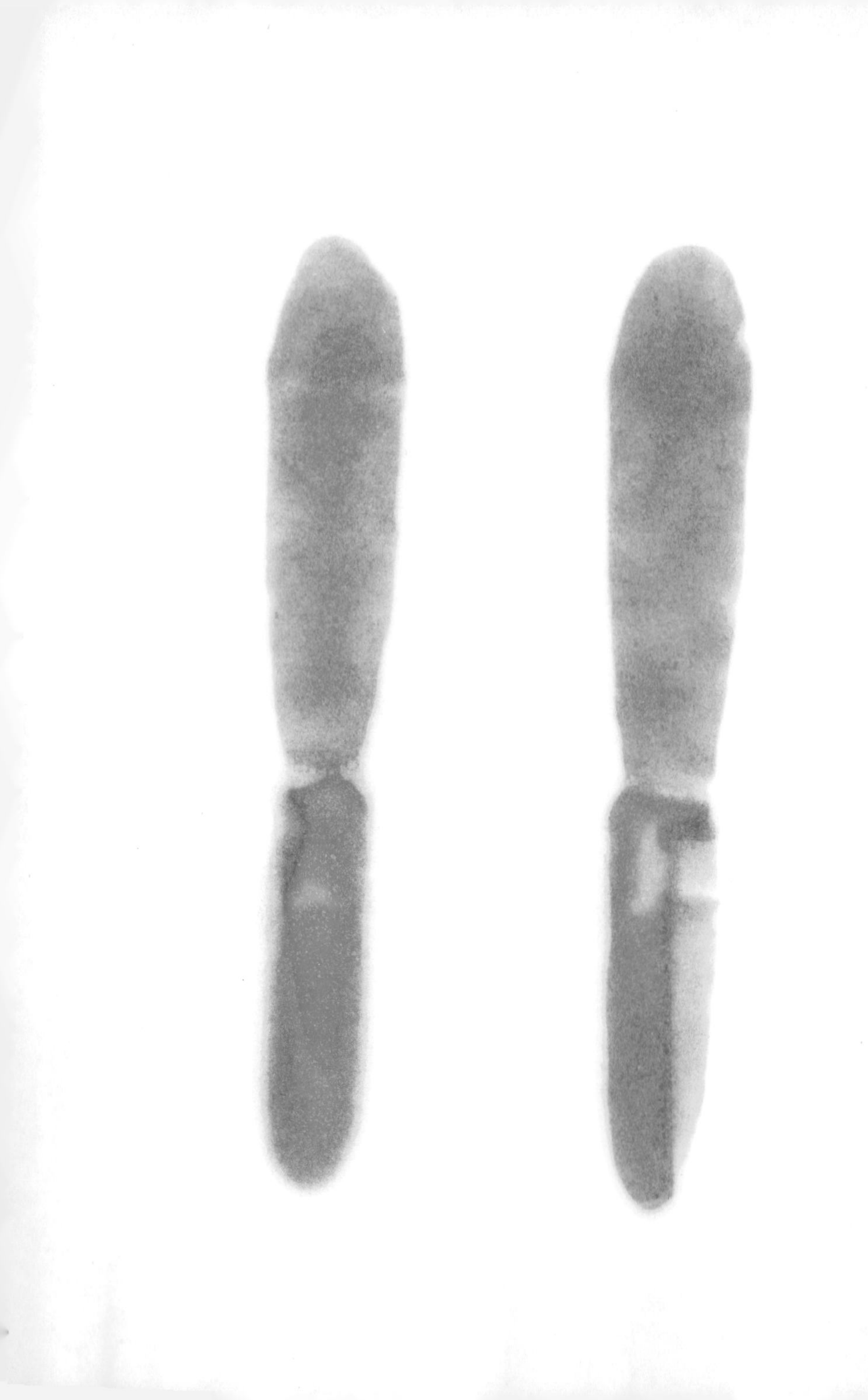

LC
573
.L78
1977
Rudnick, Milton, L.
Authority and obedience
in the church.